GROUP
COGNITIVE
THERAPY

Pergamon Titles of Related Interest

Carstensen/Edelstein HANDBOOK OF CLINICAL GERONTOLOGY
Lewinsohn/Teri CLINICAL GEROPSYCHOLOGY: New Directions in Assessment and Treatment
Pinkston/Linsk CARE OF THE ELDERLY: A Family Approach
Rybash/Hoyer/Roodin ADULT COGNITION: Processing, Thinking and Knowing
Tamir COMMUNICATION AND THE AGING PROCESS: Interaction Throughout the Life Cycle

Related Journals
(Free sample copies available upon request)

CLINICAL PSYCHOLOGY REVIEW
EXPERIMENTAL GERONTOLOGY

PSYCHOLOGY PRACTITIONER GUIDEBOOKS

EDITORS

Arnold P. Goldstein, Syracuse University
Leonard Krasner, SUNY at Stony Brook
Sol L. Garfield, Washington University

GROUP
COGNITIVE THERAPY
A Treatment Approach
for Depressed Older Adults

ELIZABETH B. YOST
LARRY E. BEUTLER
M. ANNE CORBISHLEY
JAMES R. ALLENDER
University of Arizona

PERGAMON PRESS
New York   Oxford   Toronto   Sydney   Frankfurt

Pergamon Press Offices:

U.S.A.	Pergamon Press Inc., Maxwell House, Fairview Park, Elmsford, New York 10523, U.S.A.
U.K.	Pergamon Press Ltd., Headington Hill Hall, Oxford OX3 0BW, England
CANADA	Pergamon Press Canada Ltd., Suite 104, 150 Consumers Road, Willowdale, Ontario M2J 1P9, Canada
AUSTRALIA	Pergamon Press (Aust.) Pty. Ltd., P.O. Box 544, Potts Point, NSW 2011, Australia
FEDERAL REPUBLIC OF GERMANY	Pergamon Press GmbH, Hammerweg 6, D-6242 Kronberg-Taunus, Federal Republic of Germany
BRAZIL	Pergamon Editora Ltda., Rua Eça de Queiros, 346, CEP 04011, São Paulo, Brazil
JAPAN	Pergamon Press Ltd., 8th Floor, Matsuoka Central Building, 1-7-1 Nishishinjuku, Shinjuku, Tokyo 160, Japan
PEOPLE'S REPUBLIC OF CHINA	Pergamon Press, Qianmen Hotel, Beijing, People's Republic of China

First printing 1986

Library of Congress Cataloging in Publication Data
Main entry under title:

Group cognitive therapy.

    (Psychology practitioner guidebooks)
    Bibliography: p.
    Includes index.
    1. Depression, Mental--Treatment. 2. Cognitive
therapy. 3. Group psychotherapy. 4. Geriatric
psychiatry. I. Yost, Elizabeth B. II. Series.
[DNLM: 1. Depresssion--in old age. 2. Depression--
therapy. 3. Psychotherapy, Group--in old age.
4. Psychotherapy, Group--methods. WM 171 G8815]
RC537.G76   1986   616.85'27   85-28366
ISBN 0-08-031919-X
ISBN 0-08-031918-1 (pbk.)

Printed in Great Britain by A. Wheaton & Co. Ltd., Exeter

Contents

List of Tables and Figures

Preface

The concepts presented in this volume initially arose out of a desire to design an economical treatment for depression that could be practiced by nurses in health care programs devoted to the elderly. The first effort was directed by Dr. Maureen Chaisson-Stewart under a grant from the Department of Health, Education and Welfare, Division of Nursing, with Dr. Larry E. Beutler as a consultant to the project. As plans developed and others of us became involved, the focus of potential interventions narrowed to both cognitive therapy and a group format. Our review of the literature led us to conclude that (a) depression is a major problem among older adults; (b) nonmedical interventions are especially advantageous for the elderly, given their many medical problems and the complications from them; (c) cognitive therapy is an established, effective psychological intervention for depression; (d) group therapy promises a cost-effective mode of psychological intervention.

Based upon these premises, it made sense to develop a protocol for the application of cognitive therapy in a group format, specifically addressing the problems of the elderly.

The initial efforts to develop a training program and test the interventions left us optimistic about the value of our reasoning (Chaisson, Beutler, Yost, & Allender, 1984; Yost, Allender, Beutler, & Chaisson-Stewart, 1983). Hence, a broader study under the direction of Larry E. Beutler was planned, underwritten by Upjohn Pharmaceuticals. The intent of this project was both to develop the treatment program and evaluate the efficacy of this form of cognitive therapy used with and without psychoactive and antidepressant medications. Although this study is not yet complete, the preliminary results are most promising. This book describes the protocol that evolved from the study: cognitive therapy in a group format, directed at the problem of depression in aging adults.

Our presentation here of cognitive therapy in groups follows the sequence we used in treatment. After some background on the advantages of cognitive therapy for the depressed elderly, examining the unique aspects of the treatment and the population, we address issues of diagnosis and screening, emphasizing how to determine a client's appropriateness for this form of treatment. Treatment itself is divided into four phases, which are discussed sequentially. The initial treatment stage, in particular the first session, concentrates on developing expectations and teaching the concepts required to implement the treatment. The second phase emphasizes the development of concepts and teaches participants to understand their own cognitive processes in relationship to unhappy moods. The third phase implements procedures of change, primarily to change those cognitive and behavioral patterns associated with depression. The final phase of therapy reinforces changes in behavior, feelings, and social activities and inoculation against future stress.

The final chapter addresses more general issues: the patient-therapist relationship, the use of cotherapists, and how cognitive therapy can be adjusted to particular needs and problems. By applying these concepts within the context of the group-oriented procedures themselves, we believe that a comprehensive, effective psychotherapeutic program can be established.

It has been our experience that traditional cognitive and behavioral formats need to be modified in order to provide effective intervention for older adults. We emphasize an educational approach, which relies upon direct instruction as well as exploration, and self-initiated change. We also emphasize the power of the group to provide support and reassurance and the importance of the client's ability to collaborate with the therapist and the other participants. Transmission of knowledge is an important aspect of treatment, but so is social support and the establishment of interpersonal relationships, especially in the case of older adults. Therefore, we depart from the conventional rule that clients should not associate with group members outside of treatment. While this rule continues to hold for therapists, we have found that the support and involvement of the group, outside of therapy, is an important healing force for the elderly.

This book was written for practitioners and students who plan to work with groups of depressed older adults. We have not attempted to teach the novice group leadership skills or how to work with older persons. We assume prior training and experience, so that what the practitioner lacks is the technical know-how of implementing specific procedures based upon cognitive principles. As a result, we kept theory and research findings to a minimum and present the material in a step-by-step manner. Of course, therapists still must modify the materials to fit their groups and their needs. Throughout the book, we provide suggestions on how to individualize the procedures and emphasize the need to be flexible in adapting the current approach.

In writing this volume, we are indepted to Alan I. Levenson, M.D.,

Chairman of the Department of Psychiatry, who was instrumental in helping us obtain this grant and who was a coprincipal investigator of the research project on which this volume was based. We also wish to express our gratitude to G. Maureen Chaisson-Stewart, Ph.D., for first inviting our involvement with the study of cognitive therapy among depressed older adults. We are also grateful to the Upjohn Pharmaceuticals Company for supporting the research that provided the basis for this manual. Finally, we would like to thank the project therapists: Ron Arrington, M.S., Elena Oro-Beutler, Ph.D., James Bonk, Ph.D., and Judith Lerman, M.S.W., and to extend special appreciation to Marie Jones who patiently typed the manuscript and to our students who suffered through our clumsy initial conceptualizations.

Chapter 1
Introduction

The promise of tranquility in one's "golden years" has not been realized by many Americans. We live in an aging society, 15% of the population is expected to be over the age of 65 by the year 2000. This figure is expected to continue to increase into the 21st century (Eisdorfer, Cohen, & Veith, 1980). The proportionate increase in older adults within the general population is made significant for health care professionals by the escalating rates of psychological and medical disturbances that accompany the aging process. Clearly, the status of being a "mature adult" is not accompanied by a time of quiescence and stability. The golden years are a time of change and adjustment, often made more difficult by the loss of both psychological resiliency and the social support systems that assist younger individuals cope with change. While most of those over the age of 65 seem to handle such changes with minimal disruption (Romaniuk, McAuley, & Arling, 1983), a significant number of people succumb to the turmoil and manifest both depression and loss of self-esteem.

Accurate statistics on the incidence of depression among older adults are difficult to obtain, and much depends upon the method by which depressive conditions are assessed. The confounding influences of medical conditions, increased tendencies toward hypochondriasis, and natural decreases and changes in sexual drive and sleep patterns all combine with the tendency of older adults to frequently deny or fail to recognize their own feelings of depression. These factors complicate collection of meaningful figures on the incidence and prevalence of depression (e.g., Busse, 1978; Eisdorfer et al., 1980; Kaszniak & Allender, 1985). Eisdorfer et al. (1980) conclude that the aged may have an extremely high rate of transient but recurring symptoms of depression. These symptoms, although not severe enough to satisfy the DSM III criteria for a major depressive disorder, produce significant distress and impair victims' lives. Thus, the frequency and intensity of depressive episodes might increase with age but be of too short a duration for the significance of this disturbance to show up in changing incidence rates based upon diagnosis. Nonetheless, estimates of the incidence of depression range from 20% among older

1

adults in the United States, and the suicide rate may be three times higher in the elderly than in the general population (Chaisson-Stewart, 1985).

Despite its underdiagnosis, depression assumes greater social significance among the elderly than in younger people (Busse, 1978; Dovenmuele & Vervoerdt, 1962), in part due to the high suicide rates. Men over 65 are estimated to be four times more likely to commit suicide than men under 25, the next highest peak period. Yet, major depression is diagnosed only twice as often among older people, indicating the lethality of depression in older adults (Eisdorfer et al., 1980). While suicide rates for women peak at a somewhat earlier age and are not as pronounced as they are for men, suicides occur more frequently in later years than in the first three decades of life (Eisdorfer et al., 1980).

One objective of this chapter is to consider the influence of life changes on elderly adults, and their problems in adjusting to these changes. Changing health patterns, changing medication habits, and developmental changes associated with changing social roles, loss of significant others, and social developments all bear a particular relationship to depression among the elderly. In addition, this chapter will provide a theoretical overview of some of the components of cognitive behavior therapy, to establish the groundwork for our application of these principles to the particular problems of the elderly.

CHANGES CONFRONTING
THE OLDER ADULT

Of the many life changes to which the older adult is susceptible, the death of a loved one bears most closely upon the development of depression. At any given time, 10% of women in western culture may be widowed (Greenblatt, 1978). The normal process of mourning following bereavement (i.e., loss) includes many qualities of clinical depression (Pollock, 1977). Indeed, in prolonged bereavement, the symptoms can assume all of the characteristics of a major depression and be accompanied by dramatically escalated mortality and morbidity rates (e.g., Jacobs & Ostfeld, 1977; Kraus & Lilienfeld, 1959; Parkes, 1972). The risk of mortality seems to be particularly high among men during the first year following the death of their wives (Young, Benjamin, & Wallis, 1963); among women, the likelihood of mortality following such a loss is initially lower but continues for a longer period of time (Cox & Ford, 1967). Mortality rates increase perhaps as much as sevenfold over baseline expectancies during the first year following significant loss and, at least for women, these rates may increase during the second and third years as well (Cox & Ford, 1967; Rees & Lutkins, 1967). Reviewing suicide mortality, Bunch (1972) observed that

during a five-year period preceding suicide, 36% of a sample of 75 sub-
jects had lost a parent or spouse and that suicide rates were particularly
high among widowers. Moreover, significant changes in physical health
have been shown to follow such losses (Maddison, 1968; Parkes, 1972;
Vachon, 1976). As much as a 25% deterioration in health occurs during
the first 13 months following loss, with somewhat higher levels of health
problems among surviving women than among men (e.g., Marris, 1974;
Vachon, 1976).

Anxiety, fear of decompensation, panic, nightmares, insomnia, appetite
disturbance, and other psychophysiological symptoms commonly follow
the loss of a significant other. As much as a 40% increase in somatic symptoms has been reported to accompany bereavement (Clayton, 1974; Parkes,
1972). In some individuals, these symptoms become exacerbated and account for a threefold increase in hospitalization during the postloss period
(Glick, Weiss, & Parkes, 1974).

Nearly one half of those who survive losses develop clinical levels of
depression (e.g., Clayton, Halikas, & Maurice, 1972; Clayton, 1974, 1979).
Such clinical depression may last several years beyond the time of loss,
especially if other institutional support systems are inadequate, as is
typically the case among elderly populations (e.g., Clayton, 1974; Maddison, 1968; Parkes, 1972). Partially as a result of these depressogenic patterns, psychiatric hospitalization rates increase during the bereavement
period by approximately a factor of six (Frost & Clayton, 1977; Parkes,
1972). Higher rates of depression may also account for the increased intake of hypnotic medications, alcohol, and tranquilizers that often occurs
during the bereavement period (Clayton, 1974; Parkes, 1964).

While the foregoing patterns are characteristic of loss at any age, the
increased probability of loss among elderly people greatly exaggerates the
significance of such findings. Loss contributes to increased depression,
somatic complaints, medical illness, hospital rates, and drug usage, as well
as changing sleep patterns, loss of social contacts, and decreased social
functioning. Problems resulting from loss are compounded in the elderly by changes associated with normal aging. These changes include loss
of sensory functions, particularly those that affect the perception of speech
(O'Neil & Calhoun, 1975; Orchik, 1981), the loss of sexual ability (Karacan,
Salis, & Williams, 1978), and the increased probability of such dementing
conditions as Alzheimer's disease (Tomlinson, 1982; Terry & Katzman,
1983), Parkinson's disease (Mayeux, 1982), and other neurologic conditions (Kaszniak, Sadeh, & Stern, 1985). Not only do these conditions frequently mask depression, they can also increase the subjective sense of
helplessness and dysfunction, which can in fact precipitate secondary
depression.

The effects of normal, developmental changes add to social forces and contribute to a sense of tentativeness and uselessness, which often characterizes older members of western civilizations. These societal factors include forced or even voluntary retirement, displacement at work by junior colleagues, societal movements that isolate the elderly, and the accumulation of rapid social and technological advances. Retirement communities and nursing homes, despite all their advantages, isolate older individuals from family and friends and often confine their acquaintances to the infirm, aged, and dying. In these settings, aging adults may become aware that technical advances which prolong life do not always improve its quality and sometimes make life under artificial conditions less appealing than death. Similarly, rapid and incomprehensible technological or medical advances may serve as grim reminders of their inability to keep up with and contribute to society.

To complicate the picture even further, frequently the elderly do not identify their symptoms—changing social interactions, loss of interest, declining health, and increased susceptibility to disturbance—as depression (e.g., Barnes, Veith, & Raskind, 1981). Because the elderly deny or misinterpret dysphoria, their disturbed sleeping patterns (Webb, 1982) and other vegetative signs are often treated symptomatically by general physicians. As a result, multiple medications are prescribed for symptomatic relief, a serious problem among the elderly (Eisdorfer & Friedel, 1977) and one that may be implicated in a variety of cognitive dysfunctions observed in this population (Chapron & Lawson, 1978; Hicks, Funkenstein, Dysken, & Davis, 1980). Compared to younger people, the elderly are more sensitive to adverse side effects of medications and they are likely to have a very large number of medications available to them or prescribed for them because of various symptoms and conditions (Eisdorfer et al., 1980). Many of these drugs and their synergistic effects can exacerbate symptoms of depression rather than alleviate them, particularly in view of the difficulty the elderly often have adhering to schedules and their own intake regimens.

The cultural meaning assigned to changes in health and loss exacerbates hopelessness and may decrease the effectiveness of treatment for depression. For example, Troll and Nowak (1976) observe that western society conveys a consistent and negative attitude about advancing age to its citizens. This attitude can lead to self-devaluation as people become older and can also negatively influence the attitudes of younger individuals who attempt to provide care for older adults (e.g., Lewis & Johansen, 1982). A negative view of aging and death can further result in elderly individuals becoming preoccupied with past events and seeking solace in past accomplishments. Such a retrospective view of one's life might fail to facilitate empathy among future-oriented, younger individuals in the client's social support system. A similar disparity of viewpoints might also pose problems of acceptance for providers in the health care system.

DIAGNOSTIC AND TREATMENT COMPLICATIONS

The difficulty of establishing reliable and helpful diagnoses and prescribing effective treatments is complicated by several other issues. Differentiating among dementia, depression, and neurological disorders is especially difficult in the elderly. Iatrogenic effects of drugs are not easily ruled out and distinctions among transitory depressive symptoms, depression as a normal response to loss (grief), and abnormal depressive disturbances become even more clouded. Treatment decisions also become more complex since these must attend to the attitudes and expectations that characterize elderly groups as well as to their declining abilities and changing perceptions. Well established attitudes toward "doctors," the sick role, and psychological providers often derive from previous negative experiences with the medical system. The therapist must become aware of these attitudes and develop psychotherapeutic interventions that do not reinforce these earlier biases.

In implementing psychotherapeutic interventions for the depressed elderly, for example, one must be aware of the particular cohort attitudes toward emotional well-being and mental health that often characterize those whose attitudes were formed five, six, and seven decades ago. While society has become more psychologically aware, contemporary elderly groups probably still hold some suspicion and doubt regarding the value of psychological concepts. They are reluctant to undergo evaluation by those identified as "mental health specialists," tend not to interpret their problems in a psychological way, and may be uncomfortable with or insensitive to discussions of a causal relationship between emotional well-being and physical status. The sensitive therapist must provide a framework through which such individuals can perceive their emotional well-being without stigmatizing themselves or decreasing their own sense of value.

Behavioral and cognitive approaches to depression represent such a framework. These approaches emphasize both the sense of social responsibility and individualism that frequently characterize the attitudes of elderly individuals who have been raised on a diet of self-sufficiency. It is largely for this rational appeal, combined with the demonstrated effectiveness of such approaches, that we selected a cognitive behavioral approach for our work with the depressed elderly.

Additionally, effective psychotherapeutic interventions must be designed to interact closely with and be responsive to both client medical conditions and affective states. Medical problems have a significant effect upon depression, and depression, in turn, can have a significant effect upon a person's medical condition. Close interactions among all of the client's treatment resources are required if psychological intervention is to be truly responsive to the client's needs in the face of inevitable declining health and eventual death. Such issues must be addressed in a way that facilitates client trust and confidence. That is, treatment resources must be established in a manner that maximizes rather than threatens client cooperation while, at the same time, enhancing the education of clients about the relationship between emotional well-being and health. Particular attention must be given to client consent, expectations and participation in order to accomplish these multifaceted goals. Group interactions that include other elderly can provide assistance and support in establishing the credibility of the treatment mechanism and, in addition, create stable social support systems. Friendships and social networks emanating from the group experience can have a very powerful impact on the depressed person and support the technical procedures and theoretical philosophies that underwrite the treatment.

This book was derived from our experience with the foregoing issues. It represents the accumulation of several years of experience training therapists and treating elderly depressed clients. The presentation will draw upon these experiences as much as it draws upon empirical literature in suggesting a practical approach to the group treatment of the depressed elderly.

OVERVIEW OF COGNITIVE THERAPY

Before proceeding with a detailed description of group cognitive therapy as applied to the depressed elderly, it behooves us to attend briefly to the theoretical underpinnings of this treatment modality, particularly as these concepts are relevant to the treatment of older adults.

Cognitive therapy rapidly gained prominence among psychotherapists (Beutler, Crago, & Arizmendi, in press; Smith, Glass, & Miller, 1980). Its efficacy has nearly achieved the status of a given, particularly in the treatment of depression. This status has largely been achieved by the easy incorporation of many of its concepts into the broader range of psychotherapy (e.g., Anderson, 1980) and the rapid accumulation of studies that demonstrate its power. The best-known meta analysis of psychotherapy outcome studies, conducted by Smith, Glass, and Miller (1980), revealed that cognitive and behavior therapies had the most dominant and pervasive effects of the various treatment methods explored. In a follow-up analysis of similar but more selective studies, Shapiro and Shapiro (1982) also concluded that among the psychotherapies, cognitive and behavioral treatments consistently exerted the most pronounced effects across a variety of psychological disturbances. Such reviews combine with specific studies (e.g., Beck, Hollon, Young, Bedrosian, & Budenz, 1984; Rush,

Beck, Kovacs, & Hollon, 1977; Simons, Garfield, & Murphy, 1984) to suggest that these treatments have a very persuasive influence on clients with moderate and severe reactive depressions, even when compared to the effects of more traditional, psychopharmacological treatments, whose power has long been accepted. Some of these findings contrast with the usual conclusion that psychotherapy and pharmacotherapy exert equivalent and additive effects (e.g., Luborsky, Singer, & Luborsky, 1975) and they emphasize the potential of cognitive therapies to produce results exceeding those of tricyclic antidepressants used, either alone or with cognitive treatments (Rush, Beck, Kovacs, & Hollon, 1977). Apparently, the unique effects of cognitive therapy on self-concept and hopelessness make this treatment particularly useful in the treatment of depression and these effects are not duplicated in other treatments (Rush, Beck, Kovacs, Weissenburger, & Hollon, 1982). Recent developments suggest that the power of psychotherapy in its generic form, and in treating depressive conditions in particular, has been underrated, especially compared to the efficacy of the major antidepressant medications (Steinbrueck, Maxwell, & Howard, 1983). Nonetheless, the relatively powerful effects of cognitive therapies compared to other psychotherapies (e.g., Shapiro & Shapiro, 1982) make cognitive approaches particularly appealing in treating individuals with unipolar depressions.

Mechanisms of Change

In spite of clear demonstrations of the efficacy of cognitive therapy over other medical and psychological interventions, the basis for such effectiveness still remains unclear. For example, Simons et al. (1984) failed to find that changes in client cognitive patterns accounted for relief from depression, when comparing the effectiveness of cognitive therapy to pharmacotherapies. There is disagreement about whether there are specific cognitive patterns that characterize unipolar depression (Silverman, Silverman, & Eardley, 1984), and that these patterns appear to change with remission regardless of the form of intervention (Eaves & Rush, 1984). Also, significant questions have been raised about the validity of the theory that relates cognition to negative emotions in cognitive therapy (e.g., Silverman et al., 1984; Zajonc, 1984). In a review of this literature, for example, Coyne and Gotlib (1983) failed to find strong empirical support for either Beck's model or an alternative cognitive model of depression based upon learned helplessness. Such observations have given rise to heated debates in the psychological literature about the relationship between cognition, emotion, and therapy-induced changes (e.g., Kuiper, Olinger, & MacDonald, 1983; Lazarus, 1984; Zajonc, 1984).

Ultimately such controversy and discussion is likely to clarify the way in which cognitive therapy exerts its effect. In the meantime, use of this approach rests on the strength of current outcome literature, which continues its relatively strong support of the value of cognitive therapy in treating clients with depression. This observation reinforces our selection of cognitive therapy to treat elderly depressed clients.

Cognitive Therapy Models

In spite of the literature on the general efficacy of cognitive therapy, it is inappropriate to think of this therapy as a single entity. Indeed, cognitive concepts can be invoked to describe most psychotherapies (e.g., Anderson, 1980), and a wide variety of procedures and orientations have been used to create selective and intentional cognitive change. Differences among cognitive approaches range from those that detail isolated techniques to those that entail the formulation of comprehensive theories. The approaches also vary in the degree to which they incorporate strategies and technologies borrowed from behavioral and humanistic therapies. The originators of various approaches not only argue for the saliency of their own particular orientations, but over whether cognitive therapies represent a subset of some broader theory or are a superordinate approach, incorporating behavioral and other interventions.

Most approaches to cognitive therapy have not developed comprehensive systems of application but focus on either refining the applications of isolated strategies or developing new techniques. Concomitantly, the various approaches differ in their understanding and use of client cognitions. Many earlier approaches used visual imagery to stimulate anxiety in clients instead of overt, noxious consequences. The *covert behavioral* approaches include systematic desensitization, covert sensitization, covert modeling or rehearsal, and implosive therapy. These applications ordinarily represent isolated techniques whose primary focus is upon behavioral change or subjective anxiety. Cognitive processes are used simply as vehicles to produce such change.

In contrast, some cognitive approaches emphasize systematic restructuring of cognitions as a primary objective of treatment. While these approaches continue to emphasize the importance of behavioral and affective change, they differ philosophically from the covert behavioral strategies in that their primary objective is not to give the client a new behavioral skill (e.g., relaxation or new coping strategies), but to reorient and adjust established beliefs and attitudes to make them more consistent with the demands of reality. The focus of change is client well-being, a subjective, internal state. At least three integrated approaches focusing on cognitive restructuring have been developed.

The first and earliest formalized form of *cognitive modification*, as these approaches might be called, was developed by Albert Ellis (Ellis & Harper, 1961) and entitled *rational emotive therapy*. Ellis established some of the basic foundations and theoretical underpinnings for all subsequent cognitive change therapies by emphasizing the indirect relationship between situations and the subsequent feelings and behaviors. This relationship was assumed to be indirect due to the mediating influences of the covert beliefs and values that a person held toward situations, which determined feelings and actions more directly than external events. The assumption that a situation (A) activated certain learned and often distorted beliefs, interpretations, and attitudes (B) to produce inappropriate and often neurotic feelings or behavior (C) has been maintained as a cardinal principle in Ellis' and all subsequent cognitive change therapies. Ellis went further, however, to define 11 basic irrational attitudes that he considered to be at the foundation of most neuroses and adjustment problems. These fundamental attitudes were contrasted with more rational alternatives that, Ellis proposed, could be learned in order to subsequently make the client's behavior more adaptive and appropriate.

Two major theoreticians developed alternative and almost equally comprehensive approaches that, while adopting and accepting Ellis' basic A-B-C premise, attempted to define *irrationality* in ways more consistent with the idiosyncrasies of individual clients. Hence, rather than assuming the presence of a finite number of neurotiform ideas, the approaches of both Beck, Rush, Shaw, and Emery (1979) and Meichenbaum (1977) attempted to define the cognitive structures that precipitate uncomfortable feelings and inappropriate behaviors. In his self-instruction therapy (SIT), Meichenbaum (1977) approaches the problem of change in a manner that, in many ways, coincides quite closely with that of Ellis. The major distinction between the two therapies is the role assumed by the therapist. Ellis argues that the therapist serves as a counterpropagandist, while Meichenbaum takes the position that the therapist should assume the role of advocate and teacher. Through the resultant process, which is not as confrontive as that advocated by Ellis, Meichenbaum advocates training clients to assume the role of external observer in viewing their own behavior in order to provide systematic self-instruction in coping strategies. Clients become their own counterpropagandists. The therapist encourages clients to observe the processes of their behavior and to provide self-instruction and self-direction.

Of all cognitive therapies, the Beck et al. (1979) approach to depression has probably received the most attention in recent years. More than others, Beck has concentrated on deriving a specific formula for therapeutic intervention and also has been more sensitive to those client variables that characterize different kinds of pathological conditions (e.g., depression versus anxiety or anger). Perhaps, this greater sensitivity to the type of psychopathology presented and its consistent and tightly constructed philosophical underpinnings made Beck's approach the one most frequently identified with the cognitive therapy movement by those outside the field.

Like Meichenbaum, Beck makes no effort to identify a finite number of inappropriate or irrational attitudes that characterize all clients. Like Ellis, Beck makes the assumption that correcting attitudes, rather than simply developing problem-solving strategies, is the key to changing pathological feelings and behaviors. Moreover, Beck devoted great effort and time to defining the basic structures of the cognitive patterns that underlie various types of disorders. Hence, the usual means by which clients assign causal attribution and the most frequent types of cognitive errors have been catalogued and identified to assist the therapist and client in finding those that best fit their depression. Similarly, while Beck maintains a distinction between cognitive and behavioral interventions, both are closely interwoven into a system that acknowledges the salient role of the interpersonal and collaborative qualities in healing relationships. Beck is a self-acknowledged eclectic, invoking concepts from Gestalt, behavioral, relationship-oriented, and interpersonal psychotherapies. This broad eclecticism both makes his approach compatible with many others and conveys a sense of flexibility, which appeals to clinicians in general.

Variations of Beck's approach have been explored for application in group formats (e.g., Covi, Roth, & Lipman, 1982; Sank & Shaffer, 1984) and for the elderly, although it has largely been applied in an individual therapy format (Gallagher & Thompson, 1981). While these applications of cognitive therapy vary in the emphasis placed upon cognitive, behavioral, and interpersonal variables, they also bespeak the flexibility of cognitive therapy in addressing a wide range of different psychopathologies and age groups.

Phases of Therapy

A variety of models have been proposed for the application of cognitive therapy in groups. One model (Sank & Shaffer, 1984) emphasizes the development of a variety of coping skills, presented in the context of sequentially constructed treatment modules. Clients are selectively trained in behavioral strategies and muscle relaxation and subsequently trained in cognitive restructuring, reverting to assertiveness training and other behavioral strategies in later sessions. The last modules emphasize training in integrated problem solving.

We find the use of such modules too constraining and not sufficiently flexible for the specific needs of individuals within a group. Such flexibility is especially important in work with older adults. Our own experience has led us to emphasize the importance of training clients in a few fundamental concepts, both for self-monitoring and for instigating change, and developing individually tailored, therapeutic experiences for each group member. With these cardinal and central concepts, our approach closely follows the structure outlined by Beck et al. (1979). We found within these central concepts superordinate phases of therapy, which can be defined on the basis of skill acquisition and movement of the group toward self-sufficiency and autonomy (Chaisson, Beutler, Yost, & Allender, 1984; Yost, Allender, Beutler, & Chaisson-Stewart, 1983). These are outlined in Table 1.1.

Like Beck et al. (1979), we emphasize time limited (20 sessions) treatment

Table 1.1. Cognitive Therapy (CT) Process

Activity	Time	Purpose	Content and Methods
Screening	1–2 hrs.	Select clients. Make appropriate referrals.	Individual interviews between therapists & clients. Consultation with other caregivers if needed. Present videotapes, audiotapes, and reading material.
Therapy Phase 1	1–2 hrs. & first group session.	Prepare clients for group and cognitive therapy.	Individual interviews & group interaction. Clients set goals for therapy & are introduced to the concepts and structure of cognitive therapy.
Therapy Phase 2	Sessions 2–5 (approx.)	Form working relationships. Identify client problems & dysfunctional cognitions.	Educational, group focused sessions. Uses lecturettes, self-monitoring, and behavioral techniques to initiate behavioral change, learn the relationship between thoughts and feelings, & identify individual dysfunctional thoughts. Limited contact work on problems.
Therapy Phase 3	Sessions 3–17 (approx.) Note overlap.	Change dysfunctional cognitions.	Continuing education through lecturettes focusing on categorizing and challenging dysfunctional thoughts. In vivo practice of new behaviors & thought patterns. Increased focus on individuals through contact work. Clients develop comprehensive list of personal cognitions & effective strategies.
Therapy Phase 4	Sessions 15–20 (approx.) Note overlap.	Consolidate gains. Prepare for termination.	Little or no new material presented; review of CT concepts. Focus on individual patterns emerging from lists of cognitions. Clients evaluate phase 1 goals & formulate posttherapy goals. Agenda is less structured; therapists, less directive. Clients anticipate future stress & develop change plans.
Follow-up	3–12 months posttherapy.	Reinforce maintenance of skills.	Session may be initiated and/or conducted by therapists or group members. Focus on progress made, on encouragement, and on trouble-shooting.

that can be subdivided into four phases of active therapy. Each phase is designed to build upon the previous one by introducing new skills or new methods of practice. Treatment begins with the *preparation phase*, which actually takes place independent of the group experience. During this phase, the therapist builds upon the particular problems and patterns revealed during the client selection and screening process in order to teach these clients what to expect in the course of treatment.

The preparation phase is followed by the *identification and collaboration phase*, which is designed primarily to assist clients to identify problems in their lives in terms conducive to subsequent change. During this initial treatment phase, a major concern of the therapist is to develop a collaborative relationship among the group members that will provide social support and initiate the client's active participation in therapy.

The middle phase of treatment emerges gradually out of the identification and collaboration phase, defined by the movement from an educational process, wherein the client is taught to identify problems in treatment terms, to one emphasizing the processes of change. During this *change phase*, the client is given an opportunity to experience and practice various methods of changing cognitive, affective, and behavioral experiences.

Finally, the final stage of therapy emerges gradually out of the change phase as the client consolidates what has been learned and moves toward termination and self-sufficiency. The cardinal skills taught during this *consolidation/termination phase* are methods for expanding the client's social support network, inoculating the client against future stress, and learning methods of self-evaluation. These procedures help clients determine when to implement strategies previously learned for assessing their impact.

FINAL NOTE

The model of cognitive therapy presented here is not designed to represent a final word in applications of specific treatments to specific conditions. Indeed, we maintain a broad eclecticism (e.g., Beutler, 1983) and believe that a cognitive view of depression is useful, even if not comprehensive. It is also our intent to draw upon previous work that applied cognitive therapy to depression, to older clients, and to group formats. We combined this background with our clinical work and research to provide a comprehensive framework for working with elderly clients who suffer from unipolar depression, often accompanied by social isolation, low self-esteem, self-deprecation, and fear of the future. A philosophy based upon cognitive therapy is comprehensible to the elderly, is flexible enough to incorporate a wide range of procedures, and easily can be taught and explored within the context of a group treatment program. The application of a group model holds the promise of providing the depressed elderly with a social support system and network through which they can establish ongoing relationships with others and develop the skills needed for self-assertion and self-acceptance, which will help them restore interpersonal and social contacts.

The majority of this book examines the phases and goals of cognitive therapy, along with the therapist behaviors and client tasks that differentiate them. Before turning to this task, however, we must address two very important issues—one conceptual and one practical. First, we explore in greater depth the rationale, both logical and theoretical, for using this form of treatment with depressed older adults. Then, we turn to the very critical pretherapy task of selecting appropriate clients and screening out individuals who are likely to be poor candidates either for cognitive therapy or for group therapy.

Chapter 2
The Structure of
Group Cognitive Therapy
with Older Adults

The selection of an appropriate therapeutic mode for any client is determined, to a large extent, by the client's needs and ability to respond to the type of therapy under consideration. Treatment needs are determined by the nature of the client's problems, but the person's developmental stage and life situation also strongly affect them. Response to a particular therapy or intervention depends largely on how well the client's cognitive and psychological status matches the characteristics of the therapist and of the procedures employed. While the client cannot always be matched to the right therapist, available evidence seems to indicate that, for many older adults, cognitive, behavioral, and group interventions represent reasonable therapeutic "fits."

APPROPRIATENESS
OF A GROUP FORMAT

Questions often arise concerning the response of older adults toward psychotherapy in general and group psychotherapy in particular. Family members, and even some therapists, may believe that older people are too "difficult" to fit into a group or that they require too much individual attention. In fact, as experience over the last decade with groups of older adults has shown, quite the opposite is true. Elderly people at all stages of functioning both enjoy and respond to therapeutic group activities. For example, preplacement groups have been found to help older adults adjust to independence after an extended stay in an institution (Corey & Corey, 1982); resocialization groups have been shown to be effective in returning highly withdrawn people to more active involvement with others (Weiner & Weinstock, 1979–80); outpatient groups have been observed to prevent or postpone institutionalization (Duetsch & Kramer,

14

1977); even clients with organic brain syndrome have been found to respond well to group therapy experiences (Taulbee, 1978). The wide variety of groups that have been conducted with older adults, from sexual enhancement programs to creativity workshops, is a good indication of the ability of many older people to take a productive role in group activities.

Not only is the group situation effective for older adults, it is often preferable to individual therapy, because the group offers unique opportunities that are important but often unavailable to this population: socialization, the experience of expressing one's altruistic needs, and the opportunity to be reminded of the universality of personal conditions and problems.

Socialization

Older adults are often forced to have fewer social contacts due to ill-health, lack of transportation, and the death of friends, which results in a sense of personal isolation and the loss of opportunities to maintain social skills. Older people often complain of loneliness. The less contact they have with people, the more timid and uncertain they become about their ability to talk to others or make new friends. Group therapy presents an opportunity to develop or rediscover social confidence. It is not unusual to find, as the weeks of group contact go by, that group members dress more carefully, visit the hairdresser more often, and delight in both accepting and giving compliments. While this increased self-care and interest may follow the reduction of depression due to therapy, the response of other group members seems to be an important reinforcing factor. For members who have been very socially isolated, the experience is like returning to a familiar and comfortable world.

Altruism

A group experience that fulfills only a need for socialization is not enough; older adults have an equally strong need to contribute to others. Raised in an ethic of hard work and selflessness, members of the present generation of older people value themselves most when they can help others and find it frustrating to be forced to live what they view as relatively useless and unproductive lives. In group therapy, especially in the context of a cognitive-behavioral approach, members have ample opportunity to help each other and to realize that, although their contribution may not be made in the familiar work setting, they can still find an outlet for their altruism. For example, one group member, Tom, who had spent a life of intense involvement in community affairs and scholarly writing, repeatedly expressed his frustration at having so few outlets for his energy and enthusiasm, since retirement. During a group session just before New

Year's Day, Tom read aloud three short stories and poems that addressed the difficulties of the season and concerns that had been raised during previous group sessions. The fact that he had devoted time and thought to the group between sessions, together with the appropriateness of his selected readings, brought tears of appreciation to many eyes and great satisfaction to Tom, who expressed pleasure that he was able to make a meaningful contribution to others.

In general, older adults help one another in ways that are both practical and sensitive. Offers of Christmas dinner, transportation to the doctor, and daily telephone calls to members who live alone reveal an empathic understanding of the life and needs of other people. The sense of cohesiveness that develops from the interchange of ideas and assistance is a powerful agent in combating depression, promotes self-confidence, reinforces an interest in others, and encourages the belief that there is value in being alive.

A further example illustrates how cognitive therapy can be useful in helping people meet their altruistic needs. Despite the desire to be helpful, some members are hesitant at first to offer help or advice, because of the stereotyped belief that older people don't have much to offer. Alice, for example, the oldest member of one group, spoke only when directly addressed. After several weeks, she was asked about her reticence. She revealed such thoughts as "No one wants to listen to someone as old as me," "I don't have anything to say anymore," "I'm too old to keep up with the world—I don't make sense any more." In her verbalizations, it became clear that such cognitions were not simply an expression of a long-standing lack of self-esteem but resulted directly from her enculturated beliefs about people of her age. When she was encouraged to contribute her opinions to a subsequent topic under discussion, she found that other members appreciated the wisdom and practicality of her ideas. For Alice, this single experience of speaking up in group, being heard and allowed to contribute to others' ideas, constituted substantial proof that her age was not a barrier to playing a valuable role in the lives of others. From that point on, she continued to contribute to the group and thus, incidentally, to provide a continuous challenge to her own negative cognitions about older people.

Universality of Problems

Another important function of the group is providing older adults the opportunity to see the universality of their problems. One consequence of social isolation is the belief that one is the only person in the world with a particular problem. Numerous self-defeating cognitions can develop around this belief. For example, a recurring topic among group members is forgetfulness, which many older people take as proof that they are developing Alzheimer's or some other widely publicized disease. At the first sign of difficulty remembering, they imagine that they will soon be totally helpless and will have to be cared for like children. Group members derive considerable relief from the realization that others have not only faulty memories but also similar fears and worries about the significance of the problem. Sometimes, the recognition of a common concern with forgetfulness is sufficient to alleviate much of the worry. Group members quickly accept the idea that a certain amount of trouble with one's memory may be inevitable as one grows older; a once feared event often becomes a mere nuisance to be tolerated and managed. At other times, the sense of commonality is not sufficiently reassuring, and the problem becomes material for more focused, individually tailored therapy work.

The need to realize that people have similar difficulties is particularly important because, in many cases, older adults must deal with problems with which they have no previous experience and for which their coping skills may not be effective. For example, many older women have never worked outside the home and left all financial matters to their husbands. When the husband dies, the wife is called on to learn new skills in an unknown field and may well interpret her understandable difficulty as evidence that her mental abilities are waning and that she cannot cope with life on her own. In the group, she may learn that others have had the same experience, survived it, and have advice and skills to share as a result. This pooling of wisdom around common experiences provides not only practical help but, perhaps more important, a hope that problems can be overcome.

The sense of universality applies not only to specific common problems, but to the life stage that group members share. Often, in an attempt to maintain their dignity, to avoid being a nuisance, to keep the family peace, or for fear of being misunderstood, older adults do not discuss the struggles that aging brings. In group therapy, however, it is acceptable to air one's troubles, to reveal one's fears and hurts, and to talk about both the negative and positive aspects of getting older. In group cognitive therapy, such discussions are not a matter of unproductive grumbling and wishful thinking, but are used to foster a sense of community and of intentional problem solving. With this type of sharing, a feeling emerges that "we are all in the same boat; we understand what it's like for older people."

APPROPRIATENESS OF COGNITIVE THERAPY

In conducting group work with older adults, it is important to choose a mode of therapy that accommodates the mental and psychological struggles of these people while allowing for individual differences and needs.

The concern is sometimes expressed that cognitive therapy may be too difficult for older people, in view of the cognitive changes generally associated with aging. In fact, quite the opposite is true; the high level of structure in a cognitive therapy group makes it particularly appropriate for people whose mental functioning is changing. Therapists should recognize, however, that many older adults show few, if any, signs of cognitive impairment and require no special aids to understanding and concentration (Price, Fine, & Feinberg, 1980). It is also important to realize that a slight diminution in mental ability is just that—it is not an indication that the older adult is incapable of grasping abstract concepts. Unfortunately, negative and exaggerated judgments are encountered frequently by older people, who accept such views uncritically yet resent being treated as if they are unable to think at all. Comments by several members of one cognitive therapy group indicated that one of the most enjoyable aspects of therapy was the opportunity to use their minds in new ways. They appreciated the respect conveyed by the therapists, who assumed that members had the ability to grasp new ideas.

Criteria for a Therapeutic Model

Despite the wide range of functioning that characterizes older adults, it is possible to make some recommendations for a therapy format and methods by which therapeutic experiences might best be provided to these people. For example, as a general rule, age is accompanied by a decreased ability to analyze and synthesize abstract material (Cerella, Poon, & Williams, 1980), difficulty focusing attention for long periods of time, and easy distractibility. Older adults take a relatively long time to organize their thoughts before they speak and may have difficulty retaining material from week to week (Ford & Pfefferbaum, 1980). In order to avoid inhibiting the effectiveness of therapy, a treatment approach is needed that incorporates methods to circumvent or compensate for the cognitive deficits of group members. An ideal treatment or intervention model would meet the following criteria:

1. In order to maintain the clients' attention, sessions should consist of several short segments, each with a definite beginning and end, and each accompanied by verbal or visual cues.
2. The model should include ways to cue members' attention and memories.
3. Members should have advance warning of tasks that will be asked of them to give them time to organize their thoughts.
4. Ways should be provided to assist members to retain concepts and to practice applications between treatment sessions.

In other words, a desirable treatment approach for elderly adults might resemble an educational endeavor more than a dynamic, interactional group encounter (Bates, Johnson, & Bloaker, 1982). An instructional approach makes sense on a psychological as well as on a practical level. Group members, who may be unused to the idea of receiving psychological help in a group situation, are usually familiar and comfortable with the idea of a classroom. This familiarity helps them easily make the transition to a group environment. In one group, two members stubbornly refused to refer to therapy as anything but "the class," even though other members talked about "the group;" all members seemed content with the therapists' use of a blackboard, homework, and other pedagogical devices. Such external structure may facilitate acquisition of factual knowledge, conceptual understanding, and increased performance on learning tasks (Lopez, 1980).

As in any therapy with older adults, the question arises of balance between acquisition of knowledge and skills on one hand and emotional expression on the other. However important it may be, the educational structure should not predominate to the extent that it inhibits an easy exploration of emotionally powerful material. Maintaining this balance is yet another demand placed on the leader of a cognitive therapy group with older adults.

Structural Elements of Cognitive Therapy Sessions

The structure that generally underlies group cognitive therapy serves to meet many of the needs of older adults as we have described them. Cognitive therapy sessions contain several devices that are particularly effective in focusing members' attention and in orienting them to the concepts to be learned. After the initial session, all sessions follow a similar format with distinct intrasession phases, none of which should last for more than approximately 30 minutes. The blackboard and preprinted homework forms focus the session, and frequent requests for feedback on both process and content keep therapists and members on track. Two or more cotherapists are usually used to help coordinate the presentations and group observations. Additional methods are used to help members analyze and remember key concepts in the therapeutic experience. The various skills and concepts of importance to cognitive therapy are developed and integrated logically and sequentially, from week to week, with ample opportunity for review. The most central structural elements and general organization of cognitive therapy sessions as applied to groups of older adults are described here, so that the reader will have a framework from which to view material presented in ensuing chapters.

Agenda. In the interest of both time and collaborative responsiveness, an agenda is developed at the start of each session and is posted prominently in the room. Figure 2.1 presents a sample agenda, which might be used in a typical session. Although there is value in the familiarity of a consistent pattern to sessions, this suggested agenda must of necessity be flexible. As therapy moves through different phases, the time allotted for various activities will change considerably. For example, more importance, and therefore time, is devoted to individual contact work during the change phase. In addition, the agenda, although planned at the outset of the session, may be modified during the session, as needs dictate. For example, if a review of homework makes clear that several clients failed to understand the concept presented in the previous session, the agenda might be revised to include some review and refinement of that concept, delaying the presentation of a new concept until a later session. A typical cause for adjustment arises when individual problems put on the agenda for consideration consume more time than expected. Decisions to modify the agenda are made, not unilaterally, but through collaborative discussion with group members.

In preparing the agenda, therapists invite clients to submit personal issues they wish to discuss in group, in the section headed *Contact Work.* Because the therapeutic focus of the group is on cognitions and depression, some limits must be placed on the sort of issues considered ap-

FIGURE 2.1. Typical Agenda for Group Cognitive Therapy

Date:_____   Session #_____

1. Last week's homework—pleasant activities (everyone)

                    —Jack, Betty, Sara (individualized homework)

2. Lecturette: mastery activities

3. Contact work

    —How to handle Christmas (Tom, Sol, Betty)

    —The death of Joe's dog

    —Hospitalization of Alice's husband

4. Homework for next week

5. Announcements

propriate for the agenda. In the initial sessions, and even later, leaders need to explain to clients that the ideal item for the agenda is a behavior, thought, or feeling they would like to change. Usually, this means that the item will be a recent occurrence that directly affected a member's depression, although occasionally it can be a concern from the past that appears relevant to the present depression. When items are presented, therapists should help clients express them in terms of their subjective distress. For example, a woman who wishes to add "my son's drinking problem" to the agenda can be helped to rephrase the concern as "my worries about my son's drinking."

During the first few attempts to set an agenda, clients can be expected to present unsuitable items, because they do not yet understand the criteria for selection. Thus, they might wish to discuss nontherapeutic topics, such as current events, philosophical questions, social events. They might also prefer to introduce past events about which they can complain without needing to focus on current efforts to change. When a client wishes to place an item on the agenda, therapists should ask the client if the concern relates to the client's personal and current depression. If not, can the client rephrase the problem in terms of personal, present concerns? If not, the item is probably not appropriate for contact work, and therapists can explain that, although the issue may be important to both the individual and the group, it does not provide suitable material to be dealt with in contact work. Members will be helped to select personal agenda items by being given several examples of relevant ones. It is important, when setting the agenda, that items not be discussed in any detail, simply noted for later attention.

Rounds. Cognitive therapy makes frequent use of rounds, that is, a brief canvassing of each or several group members on a particular issue, usually expressed in the form of a stimulus question (e.g., "What is your experience with ___?"). In a group of older adults, who may be reluctant to volunteer their opinions, this technique ensures that each member is allotted "air time" during the session. The client, of course, may choose not to speak and "pass." Rounds are typically used at the start of the session to discover how homework went, later to evaluate clients' comprehension of material, when initiating personal application of the lecturette, and any time feedback about treatment is desired. For example, if a client has completed a particularly emotional piece of contact work, all group members might be asked about their reactions to the work. It is not essential that rounds include all group members every time; clients should be encouraged to respond to the material in question with brevity, so that the round does not detract from other agenda items. Used in this way, the technique can be a most valuable method of involving members in the session and of keeping their attention focused.

GCT-C

Lecturette. We found it useful to present the concepts of cognitive therapy in the form of a brief lecture, delivered in a somewhat formal manner by a therapist standing at the blackboard. This form of presentation provides a change of pace and heightens the impact of the material by involving several forms of learning. Since most group members are accustomed to hearing lectures and sermons, they are likely to be comfortable in the role of listener/student and less likely to interrupt or start side conversations. This is especially true if the lecturette uses examples from the members' own experiences. Each lecturette is prepared at the start of the session, contains only one major point, takes about 5 minutes to deliver, and is followed by a group discussion, both to ensure that the material has been understood and to help members apply the concepts to their own lives. It is often helpful to provide members with a written summary of the main points of the lecturettes and to mail the summary to absent members. The chapters dealing with the treatment phases of therapy provide suggested formats and contents for lecturettes, along with examples of how lecturettes might be developed.

Homework. An integral part of cognitive therapy is the assignment of homework, whereby clients transfer in-session learning to in vivo practice. There are two basic kinds of homework: *General homework*, for all group members, develops directly out of lecturette material and frequently involves monitoring and recording clients' emotional and cognitive reactions to events or applies to the use of behavioral techniques. These assignments can, and should, be modified to some extent by altering the complexity of the task or the quantity of production, in accordance with the resources and capabilities of different members. *Individualized homework* proceeds from contact work and is, therefore, designed to meet specific, individual needs. For example, a therapist and a female client may set a homework assignment in which she is to discuss a financial issue with her husband; clearly, such an assignment would not apply to all members of the group. When either type of homework is assigned, therapists should ensure that clients understand what is being planned and that they accept the assignment as both feasible and desirable. There is no value in assigning a task that the client either cannot perform or believes to be useless.

The inertia and the negative cognitions of depression can reduce compliance with homework. This consideration warrants allotting ample time to methods designed to increase the likelihood that clients will make serious efforts to complete assignments. It is usually helpful to provide clients with a rationale for homework: they are learning new skills that require practice; it makes sense that the skills be applied in the environment where symptoms occur; there is insufficient time in group sessions to expect that these alone will be effective in reducing depression.

Clients also are more likely to complete homework if therapists discuss the mechanics of doing the assignments. For example, it is preferable to tie homework activities to routine occurrences, such as mealtimes. Regular records are more likely to be kept if assigned for two or three specified occasions, when the member can expect to have sufficient time and energy, than if either unplanned and haphazard or expected at bedtime, when the member is tired.

It is also important to focus on the client's activity or effort rather than on the end product of the homework. Further, clients need to be warned not to expect immediate or striking results, since recovery from depression is gradual, often erratic, and frequently noticed in some symptoms before others.

Finally, when group homework assignments are reduced in complexity to fit one individual's limited ability, therapists should anticipate, request, predict, and process any negative cognitions: e.g., "I'm not as good at this as everyone else"; "The therapist thinks I'm too stupid to do what everyone else can do"; "Maybe my depression is worse than I thought, and it's going to take years for me to recover." Most clients with such cognitions respond well to reassurance and an explanation that depression takes different forms in different people, that such negativism is an expected part of their depression, and that the quickest road to recovery is to proceed at one's own pace. Such clients are also assured that it is not the amount or type of homework that is most important, but the effort exerted for the activity. Therapists should not expect these explanations to be sufficient to control negative cognitions. Clients' cognitive reactions to the content and performance of homework should be checked regularly, both when the homework is assigned (e.g., "What thoughts come to mind when you think about doing this assignment?") and when it is reviewed. In each case, negative cognitions should be anticipated and predicted.

Reviewing homework is essential if clients are to consider homework an integral part of therapy. Therefore, the first task of therapists in the session is to review clients' experience with prior homework. This step has been seen as a common element in most discussions of formatting behavioral and cognitive treatments (e.g., Beck et al., 1979; Sank & Shaffer, 1984). The review is designed to assess symptom progress, provide clarification about concepts, and set the stage for feedback from other group members.

Homework review should begin with successes, however small, with all members encouraged to provide positive reinforcement for any achievement, albeit less than totally successful. Thus, therapists model both the acceptance of a realistically limited level of success and the ability to shift focus from negative to positive aspects of events.

For most clients, the homework review can be somewhat cursory; after the round of successes, examples of individual problems and responses that are somewhat typical of several group members can be addressed more fully. This intensified review might explore the client's resistance to homework or invoke the opportunity for group interchange and support; e.g., "Can anyone think of a way that might help John try this assignment?" "Is there a better way to explain it?" "How could we help you to overcome your difficulty with this assignment?"

During the early phase of therapy, homework feedback by the therapist is particularly important since clients are just learning to identify relationships between thoughts and feelings, an essential concept that the therapist must ensure is well understood. Later in therapy, the group can provide a good deal of feedback as members evaluate the adequacy of cognitive and behavioral strategies and assess their impact. Any problems with homework that appear to need further exploration can be added to the agenda for individual contact work.

Contact Work. A one-to-one encounter between a single therapist and client in the group setting is called *contact work*. The client is invited to do the work and retains the right to refuse, although in most cases the work is around an agenda item initially agreed upon by the client and therapists. Sometimes, the therapist realizes that a client is struggling with a particular issue arising, for example, out of the homework assignment and judges that individualized help would be appropriate. For the duration of the contact encounter (usually no more than 20 minutes), the other therapist and other group members are asked to refrain from commenting unless specifically requested to do so by the "active" therapist. At the end of this "mini session," feedback is solicited from the client about the meaning and impact of the work. Then other group members are asked to share their understanding of the work and its possible application in their own lives.

When clients elect to do contact work with the therapist, the work typically proceeds with the therapist's efforts to clarify the client's problem, gain permission to explore that problem, relate the problem to the event-thoughts-feeling (ABC) format, direct the client to target dysfunctional ideas, and either create ideas that are more functional or evaluate the signficance of the dysfunctional belief. The work usually concludes with the designing an "experiment" in order to test or further clarify what has been discovered during the contact work. Specifics on how to conduct contact work can be found in the chapter on the change phase of therapy, since the major emphasis on contact work occurs here.

Feedback. Feedback is the request by therapists to receive clients' reactions to any aspect of therapy, from homework assignments to a particular element of a session to the impact of the session itself. It occurs formally after the lecturette, after each piece of contact work, and at the end of each session, but therapists frequently will ask clients for informal feedback by questions such as "Does this seem relevant to your life?" "How is this helpful to you?" Will it be more helpful for us to spend time on X or on Z?" If therapists elicit feedback frequently and act upon it quickly, the effect is to increase clients' perception that the theory is tailored to their needs and that they can have a significant impact on the means of their own recovery. The resulting sense of control, collaboration, and mastery may be, in itself, therapeutic. A more detailed discussion on the use of feedback to promote collaboration can be found in the chapter on the Collaboration and Identification.

Implementation

The manner in which the structural elements of cognitive therapy usually are combined is demonstrated in Table 2.1, which provides an outline of a typical cognitive therapy group session. This outline is usually followed in all but the initial session, although some modification may occur in the termination phase. However, the structure can be modified to allow individual members to work at their own levels of understanding. Those

Table 2.1. Typical Outline of Cognitive Group Therapy Session

1. *Preliminaries* (10 minutes)
   a. Social Time
   b. Agenda
2. *Homework Review* (50 minutes)
   a. Successes
   b. Problems
   c. Contact work and individualized homework assignments
   d. Feedback on contact work
3. *Lecturette* (50 minutes)
   a. Lecturette (5 minutes)
   b. Feedback regarding comprehension of lecturette
   c. Personal application
   d. General homework assignment
   e. Contact work and individualized homework, if appropriate
   f. Feedback on contact work
4. *Concluding Activities* (10 minutes)
   a. Review homework assignments to ensure tasks are understood
   b. Feedback on session

Note. From "Group Therapy" by E. B. Yost and M. A. Corbishley (1985). In G. M. Chaisson-Stewart (Ed.), *Depression in the Elderly: An Interdisciplinary Approach* (p. 308). New York: John Wiley and Sons. Copyright 1985 by John Wiley and Sons. Used with permission.

who are intellectually more alert and active can produce elaborate examples to illustrate basic points and draw on their own experiences to create ways in which other members might apply the concepts. Similarly, homework assignments can be completed with greatly varying degrees of sophistication and thoroughness and can be adjusted to challenge members to different degrees. If the homework is presented as an opportunity for members to practice ideas presented in the group in any way that seems to fit individual needs, competitiveness and negative comparisons are less likely to occur and group participants are more likely to feel free to be as creative as they like. Thus, it is possible to respect the different functioning levels of group members without overburdening or offending any member.

Finally, readers should note that a cardinal feature of cognitive therapy is the extensive use of questions. Asking questions is a practice that addresses a variety of objectives with this particular population. The same question or set of questions is often asked of each group member in turn, thus giving advance notice to those who may need more time to organize their thoughts and who may even decide to skip their turn until they feel ready to answer. The use of questions acts as a stimulus for (a) synthesizing and analyzing information, (b) drawing attention to key issues, (c) providing an organizing focus for sessions, and (d) as an excellent device to control the pace of the meeting. In a 1975 study on the effect of questioning in groups, Linsk, Howe, and Pinkston found that elderly people increased both their interest levels and their actual participation in the group in response to the leaders' use of questions.

APPROPRIATENESS OF COGNITIVE THERAPY TO LIFE SITUATIONS

Although negative cognitions can occur at any age and quite regardless of a person's actual life situation, it must be acknowledged that, for many older adults, life in the "golden years" is attended by circumstantial changes that encourage the development of depressive thinking. As we observed in Chapter 1, loss, helplessness, and lack of positive reinforcement have been causally linked to depression and characterize the lives of a large number of older people who, quite objectively, have access to fewer options, opportunities, and pleasures than they had at almost any other time in their lives. Limited by economic, social, and health problems, many elderly individuals spend a relatively passive and sterile existence, which is fertile ground for cognitive distortions.

Cognitive Distortions
Associated with Aging

With time on their hands, few social contacts, and little energy for activities that might stimulate or distract them, the imminence of death and the need to review and reorder their lives provides older adults the opportunity to brood over past mistakes, present stressors, and future events. Hence, cognitive distortions for these people tend to be clustered in three areas: unrealistic expectations of themselves and old age, exaggerated meanings given to daily events, and changing value systems.

Traditionally, retirement has been seen as a time to relax and enjoy oneself, free of the stresses of work and family—to take it easy and do all the things for which one never had time before. To persons with such an idealized picture of retirement, the often unexpected problems of aging come as a shock, intensified by the smallest failure to cope adequately. These are, after all, supposed to be the years of wisdom, and older adults may have developed unrealistically high expectations of their own ability to adjust to new and distressing situations. Self-perceptions of inadequacy are often exaggerated ("I'm no good for anything anymore"), subjected to unrealistic comparisons ("When I was 20, I would have done this in a tenth the time"), accompanied by blame ("I should have managed my money better"), and can induce any number of similar depressogenic thoughts. Regarding old age itself, there is often a sense of bitterness and unfairness ("This isn't how it was supposed to be—I don't deserve this") and hopelessness ("It's just going to get worse, there's no point trying"). Unfortunately, many of these cries have an element of truth. The realities of old age encourage disappointment and there is no way to adequately prevent the shock of multiple losses. Older people's complaints contain an element of truth, which both evokes the sympathy of others and tends to intensify negative thinking.

Another area that fosters the development of distorted cognitions is the relative amount of time spent on various daily events. For many older people, too much time is spent on such potentially unpleasant events as visits to physicians, efforts to settle financial concerns, and dealing with family losses. In this context, the smallest difficulty often assumes greater weight than is reasonable simply because it is so time consuming. Thus, a medical report of "no improvement" may be interpreted as "I'm not getting better; I'll never get better; I'm probably getting worse but he isn't telling me." Similarly, the failure of a child to make a weekly phone call looms as "something terrible must have happened" or "he really doesn't care if I live or die." Even television advertisements, with their young, beautiful actors, can lead to such thoughts as "I'm ugly; it's no wonder no one wants to spend time with me."

Unfortunately, the values held by many of today's older adults are often another potent source of negative cognitions, once old age is reached. Such beliefs as "you are only of value to society if you work"; "you have to be independent to be a man"; and "keep a stiff upper lip and get on with the job" may have served people well during their working years but can be a considerable impediment to acceptance of retirement, during which some loss of productivity and autonomy is inevitable for most people.

Cognitive Therapy and the Reality of Aging

Although the lives of many older adults contain factors that could easily contribute to depression, depression need not be the inevitable fate of older adults. For several reasons, cognitive therapy is often the most logical way to deal with problems arising from the reality of old age.

In the first place, many of the most depressogenic factors in clients' lives are both unchangeable and continuously present. For example, one might accept the death of a beloved spouse or the loss of one's eyesight in time, but it is difficult to imagine either of these events turning into a source of pleasure or satisfaction. In the face of such unchangeable and inherently distressing life events, the most productive efforts that can be made to ward off depression are in the cognitive domain.

Second, reality dictates that for many older adults, therapeutic gains are likely to be small and variable. In the group environment, people are often observed to fluctuate considerably from week to week in their levels of depression and in their understanding and application of the concepts of cognitive therapy. This variability is inevitable when you consider that between one session and the next, a group member might have received a diagnosis of cancer, might have lost a pet companion of many years, or might have suffered any of a number of relatively traumatic events. Cognitive therapy can be very appropriate in dealing with such issues in that it focuses on short-term goals and requires clients to acknowledge the slightest signs of progress. When progress does not occur, the cognitive approach attends to negative cognitions arising out of the lack of improvement, rather than merely intensifying efforts to "do better next time."

Because older adults usually have more time on their hands for thinking, cognitive activities tend to be more influential in their lives. The elderly review past events and reflect on current ones more than younger people do. When, on the whole, these thoughts and memories are pleasant they make a valuable contribution to an older person's life, especially if the person has limited opportunities for physical activity or social contact. When the cognitions are predominantly negative, however, their very frequency increases the older person's vulnerability to depression. Cognitive therapy is thus particularly appropriate for older adults, in that it provides them with the means to control their cognitive processes at a time of life when these processes have assumed greater prominence.

FINAL NOTE

Although professionals might sing the praises of both psychotherapy and the group environment for older adults, it must be recognized that many older adults are not as enthusiastic, especially at the outset. The prospect of making oneself vulnerable to a group of strangers can be intimidating at any age, but in older adults the fear of entering group therapy tends to be intensified. Unlike members of younger generations, elderly people usually have little experience or understanding of therapy. In general, they have been raised to be independent, to solve their own problems without outside help, and to avoid "washing dirty linen in public." Rather than having a history of dealing with problems from the standpoint of emotional or psychological insight, they often have a lifetime of practical, realistic problem-solving strategies. In addition, some older adults are quite likely to have developed stereotypical beliefs about old age and, more specifically, what older people can accomplish.

Attitudes and habits such as these translate into clear, sequentially cued, and often destructive beliefs such as the following statements:

1. People who go into therapy are suffering from serious mental illness.
2. My doctor wants me to join a therapy group; he must think I'm crazy.
3. I will be brainwashed. They'll make me tell all my secrets, and I'll be ashamed.
4. I should be able to handle my problems myself. It's weak to ask for help.
5. How can talking possibly help? It won't bring back my husband or my health.
6. My situation is hopeless and is getting worse all the time. No one can help.
7. I'm too old to change or to learn new ways.
8. I've never talked about my feelings. I can't do it.

Such attitudes present considerable obstacles to therapeutic commitment and must be elicited and addressed if therapy is even to begin, much less succeed. This problem can be addressed partly through careful screening interviews and partly through the actual process of cognitive therapy itself. It is to these activities that we now turn.

Chapter 3
Client Screening and Evaluation

Experience in conducting groups for older depressed adults has led to the formulation of certain recommendations for screening that can aid in attracting to the group and retaining in therapy those people most likely to benefit from cognitive therapy and the group format. Before recruiting clients for a cognitive therapy group, the leaders must specify criteria for inclusion or exclusion of potential group members. In particular, criteria need to be established about the level and type of depression, the amount of psychological and physical impairment to be tolerated, and the extent to which those who overuse or abuse medications and alcohol will be included.

When recruitment begins, announcements both to the public and to professional referral sources should be phrased as precisely as possible, as precision reduces the number of inappropriate calls. Announcements might well include (a) the purpose of the group; (b) a list of the major symptoms of depression; (c) major exclusion criteria, for example, "This group would not be suitable for people who have a current problem with alcohol or a history of bipolar depression or schizophrenia"; (d) the requirements for inclusion, such as the ability to read and write; and (e) the number and length of sessions.

However specific the notice, telephone calls may still come from or on behalf of many more people than the group can accommodate or than are suitable. All of these calls must be processed. In addition, the list of callers must be effectively narrowed to those most likely to be suitable candidates. These people will then undergo a thorough prescreening interview by the group leaders.

It is preferable to bypass secretaries, who usually have neither the time nor the training to screen candidates. If this is not feasible, the secretary who receives initial calls should be asked to take the name and telephone number of everyone who calls, find out when the caller will be available to receive a return call, and promise that the telephone screener will get back to the caller within a specified period of time. Since many older adults are suspicious of calls from strangers, supply the name of the person who will call back.

TELEPHONE SCREENING

The telephone interviewer need not be the therapist but should have clinical skills and experience with depressed people and should have access to relevant information about referral sources. He or she should be able to make a general diagnosis of depression and assess suicidal intent sufficiently by telephone to recognize the need for emergency intervention. An ability to relate to older adults with understanding and tact is, of course, an asset. In addition, the telephone screener should know enough about group therapy to explain its purpose and function in general terms and should also be aware of suitable referral sources in the community. Suitable screening interviewers can often be drawn from the ranks of interns or practicum students in psychology, counseling, social work, nursing, etc.

It often takes a great deal of effort for an older person to call requesting help, an effort that might not be repeated if it receives no response. Therefore, the telephone interviewer should try to return calls as soon as possible. Frequently, the first contact is made by someone who has heard or read about the group and thinks it might be helpful for a friend or relative. In these cases, the caller must be asked to persuade the potential group member to call in order to demonstrate interest and answer the telephone interviewer's questions. Even if the symptoms or problem is appropriate for therapy, the group will be of little use to people who are unable or unwilling, for whatever reason, to make an initial telephone call. Those whose depression is too severe to permit making the call are probably better suited to individual therapy than to group therapy. Those who dislike the idea of a group or who feel that they are being pushed into therapy are also unlikely to feel any commitment to the therapy sessions.

The purpose of telephone screening is threefold: (a) to construct a list of callers, who will be asked to come in for a full screening interview; (b) to provide enough information about the group to allow callers to decide whether or not they are interested; and (c) to refer unsuitable candidates to more appropriate sources of help. Although there is a tendency for older callers, especially lonely ones, to want to talk at length, most telephone screening interviews can be conducted in about 10–15 minutes.

The first task of the telephone interviewer is to explain the three purposes of the call, to prepare the prospective client for the ensuing questions. Once the prospective client understands the reason for the call and agrees to be interviewed over the telephone, the screener should check out the various practical matters that would automatically exclude a person from the group. For example, does the person have transportation to the group meeting place? Will the person be in town for the duration of the group? Does the person have anything (e.g., surgery, vacation) planned during the next few months that would prevent attending sessions? Do reading and writing present a problem?

If the person is eligible for consideration, the next issue to discuss is the severity and nature of the person's depression and associated symptoms. Since many physical conditions and medications are associated with depression, the screener should also ask about current health problems, recent contact with physicians, and the number and types of medications being taken. Questions should also be asked about the person's mental health history, with specific reference to anything that would exclude participation in a group, such as symptoms of schizophrenia. The extent to which the telephone interviewer probes into the psychological state of the client depends both on the therapists' wishes and the interviewer's skill and knowledge.

If the client still has not been excluded, the interviewer should provide limited and general information about group therapy and ascertain what the person wants or expects from the group. Clients' desires and expectations are wonderfully varied. During a single week's telephone screening for one of our cognitive therapy groups, callers who were depressed and clearly eligible for the group had widely differing expectations and hopes, many of which could not possibly be met by the therapy being offered: one caller wanted a companion to share her house; another wanted help with her husband's will; others requested medication for depression, the name of a good cardiologist, someone to talk to, an explanation of bipolar depression, or help with a decision to move. Further explanation of what a therapy group can offer will help people decide whether it could meet their needs.

At this point, eligible candidates who express an interest in the group can be scheduled for an intake interview with the group therapists. In many cases, however, the person will not be eligible for the group. Should the interviewer decide to exclude a candidate, it is important to explain the reason for the exclusion and to direct the client to another source of help, if help is necessary. Older adults often are not familiar with available community resources, and many do not know where to turn when they need assistance. The telephone interviewer would, therefore, be the person's sole source of information and should be prepared to provide as much information as is necessary. Referrals need to be as specific as possible (e.g., to a specific therapist at an agency rather than just to an agency) and should be made with sensitivity to the client's financial situation. At the end of the interview, the interviewer should make available to the therapists who will conduct the personal interview all notes on those potential group members who have been selected.

INDIVIDUAL EVALUATION

Several important questions face the therapist when determining whether an elderly client is suitable for group therapy. The special characteristics of group cognitive therapy and the special needs of the elderly require careful, individualized assessment to determine the appropriateness of clients for treatment. Among the depressive disorders, for example, it is a fundamental assumption that psychological interventions are probably most useful for functional rather than organic disturbances. Even among functional disorders, however, the interviewer should be aware of the role that medical and organic factors could play in the individual's condition, in order to evaluate both the suitability and the objectives of the intervention. This is a particularly strong admonition when working with the elderly, who tend to have a variety of medical problems. The pervasiveness of medical and drug-related complications among these people does not necessarily exclude from treatment those individuals with medical problems, but one must be aware of the potential significance and complications of treatment which are presented under these conditions.

Final questions about whether the treatment is appropriate for a client are best answered through individual evaluation. Hence, the final pretherapy selection process takes place between the group leaders and the individual, prospective client. This initial evaluation usually requires one and sometimes two 1-hour sessions, complemented by additional time during which the client completes forms. Occasionally, more intensive evaluation is required and a referral for medical or psychological testing can help define the client's problem, establish a clear diagnosis, and thus to determine if cognitive group therapy is appropriate as a primary treatment option.

Three major goals guide the process of determining client suitability: evaluating suicide risk, assessing ego resources, and establishing a differential diagnosis that attends to compounding or contaminating medical conditions.

Evaluating Suicidal Potential

In the initial selection of clients, the first area of concern to the diagnostician is the client's potential for suicide. Most acutely depressed clients have probably considered or are considering suicide. Clients who are critical risks for suicide, however, are those who have no hope for positive change, who have made previous suicide gestures, who have current suicidal plans, or whose fantasies of suicide plans include actively taking their own lives. The sensitive diagnostician's first concern must be to the safety of the client. Hence, we recommend not accepting into group psychotherapy clients who are unwilling to make a suicide contract and/or who have active suicide plans or recent suicide gestures. The group process probably does not exert a maximal effect for several weeks, and very depressed, suicidally preoccupied clients might be unable to recenter themselves sufficiently to participate in group activities. Moreover, such individuals tend to resist discussing their suicidal preoccupations in a group format and might, thereby, be more withdrawn and feel an even greater sense of isolation and alienation during the initial phases of the group process. The individual interview and a careful history is imperative to assessing the presence of suicide risk. The hopelessness scale (Beck et al., 1979) is also helpful in clarifying the amount of danger present. Since part of the initial induction involves clear contracts about avoiding suicidal activities and behavior, clients who are unwilling to comply with such contracts should be referred to alternative forms of treatment.

Assessing Ego Resources and Coping Abilities

The group format requires selecting clients whose needs and goals are compatible with the established goals and structure of the therapy and excluding those most likely to either severely impede the progress of the group or fail to derive any therapeutic benefit. Thus, it is essential to assess the potential client's ego resources and coping abilities. Ego resources can be defined in terms of the client's ability to face problems and collaborate with a group and a therapist. Clients respond best to treatment if they have a history of establishing sharing relationships with others and current interest and motivation for treatment. In this, the suitable client for group psychotherapy is not substantially different from the client who is accessible to individual psychotherapy. Research has consistently demonstrated that clients who are well motivated, can establish collaborative relationships, and whose intellectual resources allow introspection are readily treated through psychological means (Beutler et al., in press; Garfield, 1978).

The question of collaborative ability achieves even greater importance than usual when the therapy under consideration is of a cognitive nature. Unlike many other therapeutic group experiences, where the focus is the interactive process among members and the expression and interplay of personality styles, cognitive therapy focuses on the identification and modification of cognitions that lead to depression. Aggressive or monopolizing behaviors, the refusal to take direction, the inability to respond to a direct question would, in all likelihood, be detrimental to group progress in cognitive therapy.

In his eclectic formulations, Beutler (1983) suggested some client characteristics that may affect the outcome of cognitive therapy: the complexity of the client's symptoms, interpersonal reactivity, and coping style. For the most part, cognitive therapy is a relatively directive procedure. Even though it emphasizes collaboration and strongly encourages clients to develop their own reasoning processes and exploratory methods, there are times when the therapist employs direct guidance and instruction in order to assist the client to develop an understanding of the concepts inherent in this treatment approach. Hence, therapists must be particularly aware of clients' investment in avoiding directive influence. Beutler (1983) defined this tendency as *reactance*, borrowing the concept from social psychology (Brehm & Brehm, 1981). Clients who may be receptive to directive cognitive therapy procedures are those who have the least investment in maintaining or asserting their own autonomy. While it is likely that any group will be composed of individuals with varying reactance levels, the therapist can keep track of each client's reactance level by observing responses to therapists' authoritative roles. The more individually focused the work, the more opportunity therapists have to adjust their therapeutic style to accommodate this reactance potential. Resistance should be an indicator to the therapist that more questioning is required and more emphasis should be placed on self-discovery.

The individual's personal style also may have some significance to the effectiveness of cognitive therapy. Clients who benefit from this procedure appear to be those who are intellectually oriented and self-reflective (Beutler, 1979; in press). Individuals who are more impulsive, less reflective, and prone to rely on acting out and projection as defenses might be less susceptible to a cognitive intervention. Certainly, such individuals are often disruptive to a group, and their number should probably be limited in cognitive group therapy.

Another consideration in the assessment of ego resources and the suitability of the client for group therapy concerns concurrent mental health problems with the potential to impede the progress of either the group or the individual. Ego dysfunctions, as indicated by hallucinations and depersonalization, might indicate exclusion from the group. Clients with this degree of disturbance often have difficulty focussing on the topic at hand and establishing rapport with other group members.

To some extent, at least, the client's motivation can be positively influenced by the therapist and by pretherapy preparation. Hence, it is not our contention that clients who initially express little interest in the process or little commitment to it should not be excluded automatically as long as they seem capable of establishing meaningful interpersonal relationships. We recommend, instead, that therapists provide the client with modest expectations of therapy, attempt to establish contracts with the client regarding attendance and performance, discuss client and therapist roles, and address directly any concerns about the client's motivation before making a final decision about exclusion.

Establishing a Differential Diagnosis

The differential diagnosis of organic versus functional disorders probably presents the most difficult task in the selection process, particularly when working with elderly individuals. Elderly people are very susceptible to a variety of medical problems that manifest symptoms classically associated with depression and that may be compounded by the negative effects of medication. In order to be maximally responsive to the client's needs, one must initially rule out the effect of medical problems that require different forms of treatment or, at the very least, would alter the therapists' and clients' expectations of the benefits to be obtained through group cognitive therapy. To restate an earlier point, this type of treatment is not suitable solely for clients with functional, unipolar depression; however, a variety of medical conditions, such as certain infectious diseases, endocrine disorders, and cancers (Whitlock, 1982), present symptoms similar to depression but are not primary depressive syndromes. Many of these conditions can best be treated through medical means.

Clients with depression, whether primary or secondary, can realize some benefit in cognitive therapy, although the amount of benefit and the specific areas of life functioning in which change will be most readily observed might be quite different. For example, primary depression may be quite appropriate for interventions that directly and primarily address cognitive distortions, whereas secondary depressions may be more responsive to interventions that include behavioral programming of social activities. In the following pages, symptoms of these various conditions will be described so that a clinician working with depressed older adults can make an educated decision as to whether a referral for alternative treatment or further psychological assessing is warranted. This section should prove clinically useful in giving cognitive therapists another perspective on cognitive dysfunction in depressed older adults. For more specific information on diagnostic evaluations of the depressed elderly, the reader is referred to recent reviews by Kaszniak and Allender (1985) and Kaszniak et al. (1985).

A major concern of diagnosis is to differentiate functional depression from other causes of inactivity, social withdrawal, or loss of pleasure.

While initially this appears simple, it is complicated in the case of the elderly. The assessment of a major affective disorder and, to a lesser extent, that of a dysthymic or neurotiform depressive disorder is based on the subjective experience of dysphoria, sadness, anxiety, and the concomitant presence of a variety of vegetative signs. These signs include appetite disturbances, sleep disturbance, loss of pleasure in sexual activities, loss of energy, loss of concentration and memory, and the presence of fatigue and diffuse physical complaints. Unfortunately, among the elderly, particular considerations make these various symptoms difficult to interpret because they are not always reflective of depression. For example, changes in eating, sleeping, sensing, and feeling occur developmentally with age and may reflect age-appropriate patterns. Unfortunately, even clients themselves might not recognize these as developmental changes and can begin to believe that something is wrong with them when they observe normal changes in eating, sleeping, and sexual drive. More specifically, lowered sleep efficiency, increased nocturnal awakenings, and less deep sleep are consistent characteristics of even healthy older persons (Webb, 1982). Likewise, age produces an increasing likelihood of loss of sexual appetites and interest (Karacan et al., 1978). These losses do not present difficulty for most individuals, unless they have either an exceedingly high expectation of their own capability or develop a concomitant sexual dysfunction. In either case, changing sexual interests and patterns do not necessarily indicate a depressive syndrome.

Concentration and memory are other examples of depressive symptoms that increase developmentally, even in healthy older adults (Kaszniak et al., 1985). Perhaps the most problematic issue in establishing a diagnosis is the observation that depressed elderly individuals frequently deny the subjective experience of depressed mood states. Indeed, hypochondriacal and physical complaints rather than subjective distress may be the most characteristic features of depression in older ages (Stenback, 1980). The significance of somatic concerns, however, is difficult to assess in this age group due to the increased probability of medical problems, including the diseases that affect mood and the depressive-like symptoms attributed to adverse drug effects.

Probably, the most difficult differential diagnosis is between depression and dementia, because the symptoms of the two syndromes overlap. A lack of initiative, loss of interest, and difficulties in memory are often found in individuals with either diagnosis. The overlap is great enough that a diagnostic classification has been created, called *pseudodementia*, that can be caused by depression. Diagnostic confusion also occurs when individuals with mild cognitive decline are depressed as well.

The initial evaluation must assess patterns of functioning that might differentiate the depressed client from the one with dementia, Alzheimer's disease, or age-appropriate developmental changes. Taking a client's history and formal psychological assessment of the clinical picture are often helpful. Kaszniak et al. (1985) provided a number of suggestions for making such difficult diagnostic determinations. Among the important clinical features that differentiate symptoms of depression from those of organic brain syndromes are the following:

1. Differential diagnostic decisions are the most difficult to make early in the course of a dementing medical condition. However, a slowly progressive onset of concentration difficulties, memory losses, and vegetative signs usually suggest the presence of an organic pattern rather than a functional depression. Clients with functional depression characteristically show a more recent and rapid onset of the disturbance, are more sensitized and aware of their dysfunction, and can concomitantly describe precipitating situations and resulting symptoms in greater detail than is usually true of clients with organic disorders.

2. The memory and behavioral manifestations of depression and dementia can also help distinguish between the two syndromes. Memory problems for the client with mild dementia are greater when asked to recall recent events or to produce new information. Well-learned information or memories from the past are usually quite well preserved in the early stages of the dementia disorders. In depression, however, memory is more variable. Often, both recent and remote memory are impaired, with memory difficulties appearing to be more selective or spotty. Unlike organic disturbances, objective memory losses, even for recent events, are not clearly documented among depressive disorders. While the elderly depressed client might have the subjective experience of memory loss, objective test findings frequently determine that memory is within normal limits, given the client's educational and intellectual background. Subjective disturbances among depressed clients can often be attributed to negative self-evaluations and to the propensity to complain about physical and cognitive problems.

3. Different levels of effort are often seen in depressed and demented clients' responses to questioning. Depressed clients often confess that they do not know the answers to direct and even simple questions and frequently avoid answering questions. The client with mild dementia, on the other hand, is likely to try to answer a question, often producing a near miss response or one that is a confabulation of information. Hence, depressed individuals will respond less frequently and in a more simplistic fashion, while demented individuals guess in the presence of inadequate information.

4. Daily fluctuations of symptoms can also be a clue to the cause of memory problems. Dementing clients often talk about night being a more problematic time for them than daytime, presumably due to loss of visual sensory input. Depressed individuals, on the other hand, usually find that

problems are worse in the morning when they have to ''face a new day.''

5. Functionally depressed clients might experience their greatest difficulty in attacking memory tasks that require effortful or elaborate cognitive processing activities. On the other hand, clients with dementia or other organic disturbances show memory deficits across tasks, regardless of the degree of effort required or the complexity of the task. The differential variability in memory problems can also be seen in the ability to recall recent versus long-past memories. Clients with mild dementia are usually characterized as having the greatest problems with recent memory while long-term memory remains relatively intact. Depressed clients on the other hand, have more selective and spotty memories, which can show up as problems in either time period. It appears that clients with functional depression are not responding to deficits in problem solving or memory skills but to their own lack of energy and motivation. This spotty characteristic is also present in other behaviors. For example, clients with depression often present great variability in performing various motor and social tasks, sometimes accomplishing surprisingly difficult tasks while failing much simpler ones. Dementing individuals tend to perform at a more consistent level across tasks.

6. Reaction to accomplishments is another way the two client populations vary. Depressed clients usually minimize and criticize their accomplishments, saying such things as ''anyone could do that'' or ''I should be able to do better.'' Clients with dementia tend to vary in their reactions. Sometimes they realize that what they have accomplished is not up to what they could do in the past, but at other times they take pleasure in doing something relatively simple or something they have not done for a long time.

7. Finally, functionally depressed clients will have many complaints about their difficulties and will often be highly sensitized to the deficits they encounter relative to the magnitude of deficits observed on objective assessment procedures. Depressed clients are usually able to detail a variety of cognitive failings with specific examples of each. The demented individual, on the other hand, usually expresses complaints more vaguely with fewer details of specific problems. While the depressed client often emphasizes problems, the demented one often will try to conceal or minimize difficulties. Compensatory behaviors, such as writing oneself reminders, are also common in demented individuals. These behaviors make it look as if the demented client is making greater efforts to cope than is the depressed client, who might appear to be complaining endlessly and to be helpless. Thus, a depressed client might be extremely upset about forgetting the name of a new acquaintance. Demented or organically impaired clients, on the other hand, tend to minimize their sense of disturbance and respond with more vagueness and effort to conceal their disability.

Kaszniak and Allender (1985) provide a variety of suggestions for the use of specific psychological and medical assessment material to assist in differentiating depression from organic conditions that mask as depression. A careful medical history, a mental status examination, neurological consultation where indicated, and formal psychological assessment procedures to clarify the nature of memory dysfunctions, problem-solving strategies, and subjective complaints should be considered in the process of establishing a diagnosis.

During the initial evaluation, additional decisions must be made about medication management. Antidepressant medication can be useful where the client is very withdrawn and exhibits a variety of vegetative signs. For example, antidepressants may be recommended for major affective disorders of moderate severity. This recommendation must be tempered, however, by the awareness that some literature suggests that cognitive therapy itself exerts as powerful and rapid an effect as antidepressant medications on nonpsychotic, nonsuicidal clients with major depression (e.g., Beck et al., 1984; Rush et al., 1977). Moreover, given the possibility that the self-directive values inherent to cognitive therapy compete with the dependent role of clients entering a medication regimen, some consideration must be given to withdrawing antidepressant medications from clients as soon as possible, depending on the extent to which clients respond to the cognitive treatment. A thorough medication review is helpful and must be deemed necessary for those taking multiple medications. This is a particularly important recommendation given the susceptibility of elderly individuals to the negative side effects that often accrue from tricyclic and other antidepressant medications. If clients can be maintained in a medication-free condition, there is less risk of compounding medical problems and depression itself with these negative side effects.

While antidepressant medications can be very helpful, particularly in the early stages of treatment, careful consideration must be given to their side effects and their interaction with other medications. The therapist is well advised to maintain close collaborative contact with a physician experienced in the use of medications by the elderly. Frequent consultation is required for certain clients throughout treatment, as medication and medical decisions must be managed and as the client's medical and psychological condition changes. This is especially true since a number of medications are used for conditions that are characteristic of the elderly and that are specifically depressogenic. Antihypertensive agents produce depression in over half of the elderly taking them (Paykel, Flenninger & Watson, 1982). Antiparkinsonian drugs, antiinflammatory drugs, hypnotics, and drugs for cardiovascular conditions can also precipitate confusion and depression. Thus, monitoring medications throughout treatment is very important with the elderly.

Chapter 4
Phase One: Preparation

In a recent review of the literature on preparing clients for group therapy, Mayerson (1984) concluded that adequate preparation not only tends to promote appropriate client involvement in therapy and improve attendance rates but can also significantly affect the outcome of therapy. This conclusion is similar to those reached in major reviews of psychotherapy in general (Beutler et al., in press; Parloff, Waskow, & Wolfe, 1978). While pretherapy induction is clearly advantageous for most clients, it is of particular value when group therapy is planned with older adults.

Extensive use of psychological services is a relatively recent development and one more familiar to younger people. Members of an older generation typically have had little exposure to treatment of a psychological nature and can, therefore, have a limited understanding of the therapeutic process or of the role they can be expected to play in group therapy. General lack of psychological sophistication can also lead older people to believe that some shame is attached to having emotional problems and can lead them to expect that during therapy they will receive expert advice and assistance, regardless of their own input. This latter belief is strengthened for those older adults who, submitting to societal expectations for the elderly, adopt a passive stance toward the management of their own lives.

Careful preparation of older clients for group cognitive therapy will train them in what to expect and familiarize them with those concepts and methods of cognitive therapy they need to understand in order to garner maximum benefits from this form of therapy. In addition, preparation allays the anxiety clients might have about participating in a group. The manner in which this training is accomplished and the time at which it occurs will vary according to therapist preference and client need, but we have found it generally effective to conduct the preparation phase in two steps. We begin individually with each client, either during the selection process or in a separate interview. This individual contact between member and therapist takes place before the first group session and, to some

41

extent, addresses itself to the seven tasks outlined in Table 4.1. The second step, which takes place during the first group session, concludes the preparation by acquainting members with each other and with specific techniques used in cognitive therapy, together with any necessary repetition or further discussion of issues raised in the individual interview. In this preinduction phase, clients might read transcripts or watch videotapes of group sessions, engage in group discussion, listen to verbal explanations, or read selected material on depression or cognitive therapy. All of these activities have been shown effective in preparing clients for therapy (Mayerson, 1984). The choice of activities will depend on therapists' judgment of client need.

The seven tasks for the therapist to accomplish during this preparation phase will be discussed in turn, with suggestions for some ways in which each might be accomplished. Since it is impossible to predict how extensively therapists might need to work on each task with different clients, therapists are encouraged to approach these tasks with considerable flexibility, guided by client need and response to both the interview and the first group session. The discussion that follows should, therefore, be understood to apply both to the interview and the group session unless we indicate otherwise.

PRETHERAPY PREPARATION

Rapport and Reassurance

Since the individual interview might be the first treatment-oriented contact between the client and therapist, a goal of the interview (and one to be emphasized throughout this therapy in general) would be to establish the beginnings of a working alliance and to allay the client's concerns about treatment. Generally, rapport develops easily as a result of the attention paid by therapists to both the individual group member and the more specific tasks of this phase. The presentation of information, the op-

Table 4.1. Tasks of the Preparation Phase

1. Establish rapport and reassure the client about group therapy and the possibility of recovery from depression.
2. Provide information about depression.
3. Acquaint clients with the tenets and procedures of cognitive therapy.
4. Explain role expectations for both therapists and clients.
5. Establish reasonable expectations for the outcome of cognitive therapy.
6. Assess the client's motivation for therapy.
7. Establish a no-suicide contract if necessary.

portunity to ask questions, and the initial one-to-one, personal contact with the therapists all tend to increase the members' comfort in the therapeutic situation. Since it is a concern that arises quite frequently, therapists might wish to address the fear of mental illness with specific reassurances. Some older clients believe that any form of emotional problem constitutes "craziness," a condition they associate with increasing deterioration, incurability, perhaps eventual permanent assignment to a psychiatric facility. Not unexpectedly, in the light of such beliefs, they fear that admitting their depression will bring shame on their families. Clients who have no experience of therapy can also hold exaggerated beliefs about this process, usually centered on the issues of self-disclosure and self-control. Therapists should be alert to the possibility that clients might hold these or similar dysfunctional cognitions, which have the potential to limit severely the benefit a client can derive from the group.

Several strategies can provide clients with some reassurance on this topic. Throughout the interview and again in the first session, therapists should provide clear information, especially when doing so would tend to counteract a negative belief. For example, data on the incidence of depression provide convincing evidence that this is not a rare problem; similarly, data on recovery from depression give clients realistic grounds for hope. Therapists should also anticipate and ask about possible client fears, rather than waiting for the client to raise them. For example, the therapist might say, "Some people think that going to therapy means you're crazy. Do you have any worries about that, or do any of your family and friends think like that?" The therapist should adopt a collaborative stance toward the client, emphasizing the client's active part in, and thus control over, therapy.

After an open-ended discussion of the subject, therapists might wish to use the material as part of an introduction to the cognitive therapy approach. The client's reaction to being in a psychotherapy group situation can be outlined as in Table 4.2, and the client can be helped to understand that these feelings are logical and to be expected given the preceding thought. Depending on how the clients react to this explanation, the therapist might proceed in any of several ways, for example, discussing further the relationship between thoughts and feelings; helping the client to identify several alternative cognitions; asking the client to judge from the interview whether the therapist seems to equate depression with craziness; or merely saying that these are common concerns that will probably be raised when the group meets.

Other concerns that arise should also be addressed overtly: "Please don't worry that anyone will try to make you discuss topics you would prefer to keep private. You will be the person to decide what you will do in therapy." At the end of the preparation phase, clients should be asked

Table 4.2. Cognitive Approach to Participation in Therapy

A Situation	B Thoughts	C Feelings
Needing therapy for psychological problems	I must be crazy. They're going to tamper with my mind.	Unsure, scared, inadequate.

about any remaining concerns or questions they have that might affect their involvement in therapy. These concerns can then be addressed either in group therapy or on an individual basis.

Information About Depression

In part to reassure clients by demystifying the nature of depression and in part to give them a rationale for the proposed treatment, therapists should discuss depression. To explain the process of depression, we emphasize the role played by loss, by a sense of helplessness, and by a negative view of the past, present, and future. We also talk about the cyclical nature of the problem and the symptoms typical of depression. Since there is a wide range of symptoms and few people display all of them, clients are often relieved to find that they do not suffer from them all. Clients are also often reassured by the realization that their own experiences are not unusual among those who are depressed and that some of their confusing and frightening symptoms result from a treatable condition rather than an insidious and incurable disease. Frequently, clients are not aware that depression can be associated with many physical symptoms, and we emphasize the fatigue and lethargy that usually have considerable effect on motivation. Discussing the memory loss attendant to depression is reassuring, too.

Introduction of Client to Cognitive Therapy

During the interview, therapists can follow the information about depression with an explanation that cognitive therapy will focus largely on the negative thoughts that both proceed from depression and increase the dysphoric feelings associated with depression. They are told that therapy will also attempt to reverse the typical downward cycle of depression by having clients engage in activities shown to be effective in dealing with the debilitating effects of depression. Since depressed clients are often unsure of their ability to accomplish any tasks at all, therapists need to assure them that therapy will be tailored to individual requirements, despite the group setting. Therapists might explain here the rationale for homework assignments, giving examples of typical assignments.

The extent to which therapists explain the various concepts and procedures in the interview will depend largely on clients' interest and ability to grasp abstract concepts, as well as on the time available. One purpose of the explanation is to give clients enough information about what will be happening in group therapy to allow them to decide whether they are interested in this form of treatment. Another purpose is to allow the therapists to judge from the client's response whether this treatment is appropriate. As a general rule, we would advise therapists to provide the least amount of theoretical information that will achieve these goals, since most clients will gain a far greater understanding of the therapy by experiencing it than by hearing about it.

It is sometimes helpful to have clients read material such as *Coping with Depression* (Beck & Greenberg, 1974) before they arrive at the first group session. Therapists are cautioned, however, that, in our experience with older adults, reaction to such material has been mixed. While highly functioning clients find the article valuable, others might find it confusing and can develop negative cognitions about their ability to understand the proposed therapy. In order to forestall this possibility, the article can be presented as optional reading, which will be explained in detail during group sessions.

Role Expectations

Therapists cannot take for granted that all clients will understand the cardinal assumption that the goal of therapy is the active management of one's own life. It is advantageous, therefore, to state explicitly that group members will be expected to take an active part in dealing with depression, and that they will also be expected to address their own personal problems, and not just those of others. The therapists will function as teachers, leaders, and collaborators but will not provide ready-made solutions for client problems. The relationship between therapists and group members resembles more a working partnership than the typical physician-patient relationship. In order to explain cognitive therapy more clearly, it can be helpful to use videotapes or transcripts of group sessions. During the interview, clients should be presented with a brief overview of cognitive therapy rather than a detailed account, which might prove confusing or overwhelming. They can be asked to regard the first group session as a time when they will receive greater instruction and will have further opportunity to ask questions.

Outcome Expectations

Since the issue of expectations is highly individual and can take considerable time, an individual preparatory interview allows greater exploration of this topic. Expectations will be briefly touched on again during the first group session. Older adults often have many concerns other than depression and might expect the group to function as a general agency for help and advice. Those people who are indeed not interested in cognitive therapy or in group therapy can be redirected during the initial screening, but even those who are accepted into the group need to understand that group cognitive therapy does not attempt to address all concerns. Prospective group members should be told that therapy will focus on depression, and that therapists will be able to refer clients to other sources of help, if necessary, for issues that cannot be handled in group.

Regarding depression itself, therapists should discuss the progress that clients can reasonably expect to make in group. According to Lieberman, Yalom, and Miles (1973), group members tend to become group casualties when they begin therapy with unrealistically high or low expectations of what they might accomplish through the group. Thus, it is important for therapists to assess what voids clients hope to have filled by the group, or what level of functioning they expect by the end of 15–20 weeks. If clients have been depressed for a long time, the therapist can point out that it would be unreasonable to expect total recovery in a relatively short space of time. Older clients, in particular, might hope that the group will restore them to a state of energy and enthusiasm they have not experienced since their youth. The unlikelihood of this restoration will often be appreciated by the client if the therapist simply summarizes and paraphrases the client's own words. If the client appears to have unrealistic hopes for the group, therapists can ask directly: "How likely is it that, 4 months from now, you will be feeling as cheerful and social as you did when your children were young and you were living near your good friends?"

Setting realistic expectations is a delicate matter, since therapists must avoid moving to the other extreme and convincing clients that very little can be accomplished. A useful approach can be to persuade clients to view group as a beginning rather than as an end. For example, one can ask, "Given how bad you feel now, what small improvements in your depression would make you feel that you were on the road to recovery?" or "If you were now at the end of group, what sort of progress toward recovery would you be satisfied with?" An even simpler question is, "How will you know you are getting better?" By exploring such questions, clients might come to accept as evidence of progress such tangible, and probably attainable, changes as one or two more social activities per week, fewer bouts of crying, a return to a former volunteer or work activity.

Client Motivation

It is not conducive to group cohesion to have several uncommitted members attend the first session on a trial basis and then drop out, so therapists should address the issue of commitment to the group individually with clients, making appropriate referrals for those people who appear to lack sufficient interest and motivation to benefit from the group. This may be a difficult matter to judge, since depressed people seem generally apathetic and unenthusiastic and are inclined to express negative attitudes. One would not want, therefore, to dismiss as unmotivated, clients whose hesitation and doubt about the effectiveness of therapy and their own ability to complete the course result from their depression. A more useful approach is to focus on client statements that might indicate a stubborn disbelief in principles that underlie the cognitive approach. A discussion both of obstacles to therapy and the clients' willingness to overcome them might reveal the clients' level of motivation. Other signs of poor motivation might be observed in repeated requests for medication instead of therapy or a refusal to consider the role of personal effort in recovery from depression. In these cases, either individual therapy or a different form of treatment might be of more value to the client.

Before the individual interview is completed, clients should be asked if they feel they can make a commitment to attend the 20 group sessions and if they are willing to keep a somewhat open mind and give the therapy a try. Clients' answers to this request should provide further indication of their motivation.

No-Suicide Contract

The establishment of a no-suicide contract with a severely depressed client is a matter of common practice and should be negotiated during the individual interview, before group sessions start. The question of whether to include currently suicidal clients in the group must essentially be made by the therapist. There is no inherent reason to believe that a severely depressed client cannot gain from group participation, but undoubtedly such a client would require careful monitoring throughout the group. Therapists might also decide to exclude a suicidal client who, in their judgment, would have a deleterious effect on other members of the group.

CONDUCTING THE
INITIAL SESSION

Both the emphasis on cognitions and the structure of group cognitive therapy are likely to represent, for most participants, an unfamiliar approach to addressing emotional problems, despite their brief introduction to cognitive therapy principles during the pretherapy interview. It is appropriate, therefore, to consider the initial group meetings as part of the preparation phase. The primary objectives of this session are (a) reinforcing preinduction role expectancies, (b) initiating the process of group cohesiveness, and (c) providing members with a didactic and experiential introduction to cognitive therapy. To help achieve this last objective, it is recommended that the initial session approximate the format of later sessions, with the addition of specific preliminary activities and explanations regarding the content and purpose of the various structural elements of the therapy.

Preliminaries

Since it is not uncommon for older adults to arrive as much as an hour early for the first session of a group, arrangements should be made to handle early arrivals; ideally, a waiting room in which participants can visit with one another. Such an arrangement is often therapeutic, as it extends the time of the group, decreases the tendency for members to use group time for socializing, and allows members to develop a cohesive support network. If therapists also make a point to arrive early, the resulting extension of the therapy time provides an opportunity for members to relate to the leaders in less formal ways and to feel welcomed as individuals rather than merely as clients in a group. A handshake on arrival and departure represents a familiar social pattern for many older adults, thus decreasing anxiety, especially on this first occasion of meeting.

Before the session begins, the time that the group will end should be repeated and any difficulty with transportation should be addressed, in order to reduce members' anxiety about keeping others waiting or possibly missing a ride home.

First Session Agenda

Once the members are seated, the next task is to discuss the agenda for the day. In later sessions, the group might develop the agenda at this point, extending it as material develops out of the homework review. Obviously, no such review can begin this first session. Before proceeding to set the day's agenda, leaders should provide a rationale for the activity and should explain how the group members will be asked to participate in setting the agenda in future sessions. Examples of appropriate personal agenda items can be provided; i.e., ones pertaining to recent events affecting depression. Since this is the first session, the agenda usually is set by the therapists, and should be written on the board as follows:

1. Introductions
2. Expectations
3. Lecturette
4. Homework
5. Feedback
6. Summary of therapy

Leaders should acknowledge that many of these items might be obscure, and that this first session will involve both an experience of the items and an explanation of their inclusion.

Introductions

After the agenda has been set, the group begins with a brief round of introductions. First, the leaders introduce themselves in order to model both the kind of information that is expected and the brevity that will allow this section to be completed fairly rapidly. Since one of the purposes of the introductory round is to enable each member to have a successful first experience in speaking to a group without embarking on depressive material, the leaders' modeling might focus on relatively nonthreatening personal material, such as marital status, children's names, hobbies. We found that a nondisclosing stance by therapists tends to increase distance and distrust in the group. Although therapists are cautioned about excessive self-disclosure, shared background may well facilitate trust (Beutler, 1983). When the participants are asked to introduce themselves, we found it helpful to provide a choice of several quite specific stimulus prompts, such as, "Please tell us what you like to be called, how long you've lived in town, what sort of family you have, and how you spend most of your time these days."

After the introductory round, leaders might wish to offer some information about their professional work to the group and respond to members' questions about the leaders. A typical question concerns the leaders' interest and purpose in working with older adults. Before moving to the next agenda item, leaders should take this opportunity to tell members that what they have just completed is called a *round* and explain both the reasons for rounds and the brief and focused manner in which they need to be conducted. The technique of rounds should be used several times during this first session, to allow participants to become accustomed to the practice and to speaking up in the group. The therapist will need to develop ways either to solicit more from clients or to contain them during rounds.

Expectations

The behavior expected of clients in a cognitive therapy group, already presented briefly during the pretherapy interview, will be repeated and discussed during the first session. These norms include the expectation that members will discuss their own personal problems, not just the problems of other people, and that they will make a commitment to change, rather than simply waiting for the leaders or other group members to provide answers to problems. Members are also reminded that they are expected to attend every session, even if they do not feel like making the effort, unless attendance is absolutely precluded by an unavoidable circumstance, such as illness. The role of depression in reducing motivation and activity can be emphasized here. Although these points have been covered individually, misunderstandings can arise and the issues bear group discussion.

Three additional points are to be covered with group members at this juncture: contact work should be described, and issues relating to self-disclosure and confidentiality should be presented. The point should be made that although members will be expected to discuss their personal problems, they will not be coerced into disclosing more information than they are ready to provide at any particular time. Leaders should also explain that it is the custom in therapy groups for the group members to agree not to repeat anything that occurred in the group to anyone outside the group, in order to help people feel safe disclosing personal material. As privacy is frequently highly valued by older adults, considerable discussion is often provoked by the topic of confidentiality and by exploration of what material is appropriate to raise in group. At the conclusion of this discussion, therapists might ask participants the extent to which they agree with the norm of confidentiality, considering group therapy's built-in limitations on confidentiality (i.e., although leaders can control their own confidentiality, they cannot guarantee that of the members).

Participants should be asked if they have any suggestions about structure that they would like to add to the list. In this first session, the rules most commonly added are likely to concern such practical issues as bathroom breaks and smoking.

In addition to therapists' expectations of clients, group members have their own hopes about what they will achieve as a result of the therapeutic experience. Since the topic has already been discussed in the pretherapy interview, it can be hoped that clients will arrive at the first session with reasonable expectations of group cognitive therapy. A valuable exercise during this session is to have members share these expectations with other group members. One way to do this is to ask members to set personal goals, related to their depression, that they would like to meet by the end of the group sessions. This goal setting accomplishes several purposes. It allows people to talk about their depression and share personal material with the group in a manner that discourages rambling and self-pity, while instilling hope for a better future. It exemplifies to members the fact that, although this is a group experience, therapy will be individualized. Finally, and perhaps most important, it allows therapists to check for unrealistic hopes and lead all members toward an end that they can reasonably expect to reach.

Typical goals will vary considerably from "I'd like to get through the day without crying" to such global wishes as "I'd like to be my old self again." In the case of goals that are vague or general, therapists should ask members to explain how such a goal would make itself apparent in daily life. If the answer to that question indicates that the person expects to be restored to a level of functioning that is unrealistic, both the therapists and the other group members can help the person to assess whether such recovery is likely. Frequently, the goal can be phrased in more realistic terms simply by the addition of a qualifier; e.g., "I'd like to feel *more* like my old self" or "I'd like to feel that *something* was worth living for." The most important aspect of goal-setting is that group members do not set themselves up for failure and disappointment by aiming for an unattainable level of recovery from depression.

Lecturette

Therapists might decide to devote most of the first session to getting acquainted and to general discussion, thus leaving no time for participants to experience a lecturette. In this case, therapists should prepare members for future sessions by explaining briefly the purpose and format of lecturettes and the role played by members in listening and responding to them.

Should the therapist decide to present a lecturette, an appropriate first choice would be the relationship between thoughts and feelings. Since this is a crucial concept, therapists should not expect that this first presentation of the idea will be sufficient to ensure understanding by all group members. If the therapists judge that the functioning level of the group mitigates against the presentation of a purely cognitive concept, other possibilities for this first session are lecturettes on behavioral techniques, which are described in the next chapter.

Homework

If a lecturette has been presented, the homework will be derived from that material. In the absence of a lecturette in the first session, therapists might assign any preliminary self-monitoring activity in which clients are asked to examine some aspect of their depression. The rationale for homework should be provided, the assignment for the next week and the mechanics of completing it explained, any concerns about the homework elicited and resolved, and agreement by clients to at least attempt the assignment should be obtained.

Feedback

Leaders can now point out that they have been asking group members throughout the session if various activities make sense to them and if they believe they will be able to participate in these activities. This process can be defined as *feedback*, and the rationale for the activity explained. Clients should be encouraged to provide feedback even if not solicited by therapists. Finally, therapists should solicit feedback from the participants on the initial session. Group members might, for example, describe what happened for them during the group, or what they liked or disliked about the session. The most likely response, as it is the most socially acceptable one, is that everything was just fine and that they liked the group a lot. At this point such general statements are acceptable, but leaders might want to set the stage for the possibility of negative reactions in later sessions by a comment such as, "I'm glad things seemed to go well today, and that we got off to a good start. However, this is not always the case, and if we are to be of most help to you in overcoming your depression, it is important that you let us know anything about the sessions that is not of value or that is not clear." In later meetings, leaders will attempt to elicit more specific comments and opinions, both positive and negative. Any complaints about the group content or process should be handled, if possible, before the session ends or at least tabled to the next session.

Summary of Therapy

It is sometimes appropriate in this first session for therapists to provide clients with an overview of the remaining 14–19 group sessions, although there is no need to do so unless clients express an interest. The overview would involve a brief explanation of the phases of therapy, both their timing and content, without too rigid a structure. Members might be told, for example, that for the first few weeks the focus will be on understanding the variety of situations, thoughts, and feelings that members have relating to their depression, since everyone experiences depression in different and highly individual ways. During this time, people will be asked to make some small changes in their daily lives that, it is hoped, will begin to alleviate their depression. Once people understand how their thoughts and feelings are related, the majority of the remaining sessions will be spent on learning ways to change attitudes and thoughts that bring on or intensify depression. Group members will also be asked to continue making other practical efforts outside of therapy sessions. During the last few weeks of group, the main focus will be on discussing how people can manage their lives once group is over so that they continue to reduce any remaining depressive symptoms and may prevent their recurrence.

Concluding the Session

It is important to conclude this first, as well as all subsequent sessions, on time because of potential transportation problems. A formal leave taking at the door, including a personal comment to each member, clearly signals the end of the session and finishes the day's meeting on a positive and socially pleasant note.

If the induction phase was successful, clients should be adequately prepared to begin therapy by the conclusion of the first group session. They will understand what is expected of them as group members, will believe that they can adequately perform their role in group, and will expect that their performance is likely to result in some therapeutic gain. Mayerson (1984) indicated that success in this phase is more likely if preparation is individualized, personalized, and allows for clients to discuss and question matters of concern relating to therapy. The two-step process we described in this chapter provides an adequate basis for pre-therapy induction, but therapists will recognize that the process will not be completed to the same extent in all clients. While it is important to move on to therapy proper, some of the concerns of the preparation phase may well arise again later and will need to be dealt with at that point.

Chapter 5

Phase Two: Collaboration and Identification

The collaboration/identification phase of cognitive therapy follows client preparation and usually occupies from five to eight sessions. The goals of this stage of treatment are threefold: (a) to establish a sense of collaborative support among therapists and group members, (b) to help clients identify the nature of their problems within a cognitive therapy framework, and (c) to initiate behavioral change in clients' lives. In this chapter, we discuss each of these goals in detail, paying particular attention to the specifics of achieving them in a group setting. We include examples and descriptions of lecturettes and behavioral techniques appropriate for use in this phase.

COLLABORATION

Collaboration, as employed in cognitive therapy, refers to the establishment of a working partnership between therapists and group members. This is actually the most important goal of the phase, since change effected by the therapist more often accrues from positive characteristics of the treatment relationship than from the specifics of the intervention (Parloff et al., 1978; Beutler et al., in press; Lambert & DeJulio, 1978). There are two aspects to this particular goal: to create a sense of acceptance among group members and therapists, and to establish a collaborative relationship by soliciting and responding to client feedback about the therapy.

Regarding the first aspect, it is imperative in this early stage of treatment that clients feel accepted by the therapists and that they become known in the group in a way that encourages a sense of mutual support and cooperation. One way therapists can assist in this aim is by reframing clients' concerns and behavior in a manner likely to promote the empathy rather than the hostility of the group. Thus, for example, a client who complains frequently of physical difficulties could be viewed as a person suffering from the loss of capabilities that are important to self-esteem rather than as a "complainer." Similarly, group members who are irritated by an attention seeker can be led to view the person as lonely and in need of human contact.

Acceptance within the group can be further promoted by allowing clients, during this initial phase of treatment, to share with each other their descriptions of experiences that justify, reinforce, or validate their depressed mood. These stories often help establish an expectation of openness and self-disclosure in interaction, even though in later stages therapists must control and limit the amount of nonfocused sharing.

A potential barrier to members' feeling accepted by the group is the presence of unexpressed concerns about the group format and the therapists themselves. Therapists need to give special consideration to the probability that elderly depressed clients will be somewhat skeptical of the therapists' ability to help, coming, as they do, from a different generation and background. Therapists would be well advised to respect and directly address this issue of age and experience differences. A statement acknowledging that some clients might have trouble understanding how a younger person can help, and an invitation to discuss the issue if it is of concern, frequently breaks the ice on this obstacle. Even if doubts still linger in clients' minds, there will be little doubt about the therapists' openness about things that could affect the group. Since the age issue can persist and cause problems, we address it in further detail in Chapter 8 as we discuss the group process. Respect for client fears or concerns can also be demonstrated in other ways, such as explaining the techniques to be used, providing a rationale for each procedure, and gaining client permission before discussing topics that could be sensitive.

While the foregoing suggestions can help promote support and acceptance in the group, the positive role of active listening, attentiveness, and the encouragement of open expression cannot be overemphasized. Such behaviors by the therapist are not only therapeutic of themselves, but provide important modeling to group members about how to respond to each other.

Client feedback about therapy also is of major importance in establishing and maintaining a collaborative relationship. Therefore, feedback is requested at points designated on the agenda as well as at times when the therapists need input from the group members. In cognitive therapy, therapists frequently ask clients which of several directions they would like therapy to take. They might be asked to help create the agenda for each session, to decide whether they wish to address a particular issue at this point in time, or later or not at all, to choose whether to do individual contact work, or to choose whether to ask for group help. Thus, very little happens in therapy without the permission or instigation of an individual or the group. Problems arising when the group's wishes clash with the overall goals of cognitive therapy will be addressed in Chapter 8.

Feedback can also be evaluative, meaning that clients are asked to react to therapy in terms of its usefulness for their situation. For example, at the formal points of feedback, the therapists ask how well clients have understood both the material in the lecturette and the application of this material to their own lives. Generally, this type of evaluation is an integral part of the lecturette itself. A review of homework should include questions soliciting feedback, "In what way, if any, did this homework help you to feel less depressed this week?" "How can you see these concepts being of help to you?" Similarly, when individual contact work has been completed during a session, it is advantageous to ask other group members for their reactions, using directed questions such as, "What did you learn from John's work that you might be able to use for yourself?" "What sort of negative feelings and thoughts occurred to you during this week?" Probably, the most frequently asked feedback questions are "Is what is happening here being helpful to you" and "How could we make this more helpful?"

IDENTIFICATION

The second major goal of the early phase of therapy is to help clients identify their problems within the framework of cognitive therapy, so that they are prepared to begin the change phase of therapy. Essentially, identification consists of monitoring dysphoric feelings along with the thoughts and situations that precede and cause those feelings. As clients are taught to observe these relationships, they are also taught to recognize and label dysfunctional thoughts. This is a considerably more complex task than might be imagined. Since most people, including and perhaps especially elderly adults, are unlikely to be accustomed to systematic introspection, it takes time and effort to reach the point where each client is able to construct a written list of his or her own dysfunctional cognitions and the events that typically precipitate them.

The principal technique for achieving the goal of identifying dysfunctional cognitions is the use of columnar records, which is taught early in treatment and continues to be used through all phases of therapy. The first step in teaching this technique is to ask clients to identify times during the week when they experience a dysphoric mood and to identify both the feeling state (the mood itself) and the situation they believe occasioned the mood. Initially only two columns are used (see Table 5.1). Many clients tend to believe that their depression is all pervasive, resembling a permanent state of being, and they are initially unable to identify specific

Table 5.1. Examples of Two-Column Records

A Situation	C Mood/Feelings
Accident on TV news	Worried, sad
Granddaughter graduates	Alone, old, empty
Plays bad game of cards	Useless, stupid, scared

moods or to notice specific occurrences that heighten feelings of sadness and despair. Therapists who are knowledgeable about common precipitators of depression in the elderly can encourage the identification process by asking such questions as, "How much worse do you feel when you find yourself unable to perform a task that was easy for you just last year?" "What happens to your depressed feelings when you read in the paper about the death of an old friend?" Other group members, who have managed to complete the assignment, can be asked to share examples of their homework and help prompt people to think of times that are likely to increase feelings of depression.

Not until the two columns can be completed satisfactorily as a homework assignment and the appropriate lecturettes have been presented are group members asked to complete a third column. This third column introduces the thoughts that connect the situations to the feelings, as illustrated in Table 5.2.

Usually, considerable direction is required to help clients identify (a) any thoughts at all that precede the feelings, (b) those thoughts that particularly relate to the unpleasant feelings, and (c) the effects of these thoughts as dysphoria. The automatic nature of depressogenic cognitions makes it difficult for clients to "catch" their thoughts, especially during the days between sessions when they are without therapist help. In order to help them catch these dysfunctional but unrecognized thoughts, clients might be asked to replay a distressing situation aloud, in slow motion. They

Table 5.2. Examples of Three-Column Records

A Situation	B Thoughts	C Feelings/Mood
Can't find gas bill	I'm losing my mind. I can't remember where I put things any more.	Frantic, lost, confused
Doctor says eyesight is worse	There's nothing to live for if I can't see.	Hopeless, tired, want to give up
A sunny day	Life used to be fun, but no more.	Depressed
Feeling down	I should be able to snap out of this.	Guilty

might also be asked to imagine or create thoughts and images that will bring on or intensify the feeling. Therapists could also ask what conclusions clients draw about a situation, in order to elicit negative thoughts. For example, a client insisted that her son's failure to write was the cause of her sadness. When prompted about the meaning she attached to her son's behavior, she realized that she was concluding that he did not care about her. Questions such as "And what does that prove?" "How do you interpret that?" "What does it mean when . . . ?" can be helpful in getting clients to attend to their automatic thoughts. Should difficulties in identifying automatic thoughts persist, other group members might be asked to guess at possible expectations, fears, worries, or other cognitive responses to the situation that could have produced the feelings.

If clients create a stream-of-consciousness report of every thought that preceded their feelings, including those clearly irrelevant to the emotion, they can be guided to evaluate each thought in terms of its possible connection to the target emotion. For example, therapists can ask, "When you thought about what you wanted to eat for breakfast, did that make you feel any worse or any better?" Alternatively, clients with a long list of cognitions might be asked to identify the two or three that they believe occur most often or contribute the most to their dysphoric mood.

Throughout this phase, therapists will do contact work with individual clients, though not with the frequency that this technique will be used in ensuing phases. In this early phase, contact work is not designed to produce change but to help the client identify cognitive structures and understand the connection between thoughts and feelings. It should be explained to clients that although this step is a necessary antecedent to change, it cannot be expected to provide significant relief of emotional distress. In this phase, the therapist is content to allow the group process to account for any emotional relief that occurs, expecting that specific techniques for cognitive change will carry the burden for long-term effects as therapy enters the middle and final phases of active treatment. Contact work is conducted during this phase mainly with those clients who are having difficulties, such as inability to identify specific situations, or depressogenic thoughts, or negative cognitions about homework. Since clients are usually unfamiliar with the cognitive approach, and at the same time often eager to receive advice with practical problems, it can be difficult to maintain a cognitive focus in this early contact work. Therapists need to ensure, however, that the time for one-to-one contact is used appropriately from the start, in order to set the pattern for the more extensive use of contact work later. Clients may need to be reminded of the purpose and focus of contact work and gently kept on track.

On the whole, contact work does not differ in this phase from work that therapists do with the whole group. That is, the client is first asked to recall a specific situation when dysphoria was experienced. The therapist then guides the client through the situation, using whatever imaging or questioning techniques that best elicit, first, the dysfunctional feelings and, second, the contributing dysfunctional cognitions. The therapist ascertains that the client acknowledges the relationship between the thoughts and feelings by asking questions such as, "Does it make any sense to you that, if you think these thoughts, you might feel this way?" Time permitting, the client can be taken in this way through several incidents. At any point, the therapist can request help from the group, although members should not be allowed to volunteer unsolicited comments. When contact work is completed, the therapist might, with the collaboration of the client, design an individualized homework assignment. Finally, the therapist asks for feedback from both the individual client and other group members concerning the meaning and relevance of the contact work.

Once identified, dysfunctional thoughts continue to be monitored via homework assignments using the three column record, in order for the therapist to determine the pervasiveness in the client's life of specific dysfunctional thoughts and more general dysfunctional automatic patterns (e.g., Beck et al., 1979). Building on both homework assignments and the concepts described in *Coping with Depression* (Beck & Greenberg, 1974), which was distributed during the preparation phase, the therapist can assist clients to identify key words and feelings that will cue them to the presence of dysfunctional thoughts.

Throughout this phase, therapists will find it invaluable to keep a running list of typical trigger situations and dysfunctional thoughts for each group member. In time, this list will provide a portrait of the client's cognitive errors and basic schema and will help both client and therapist select the most relevant cognitions to target during the change phase. By using this list, the therapist will also be in a position to recognize whether a particular issue arises frequently for the client or is a relatively infrequent, and perhaps insignificant, event that may not warrant therapeutic attention.

As clients develop their individualized lists of negative thoughts, therapists, and sometimes clients too, will notice repetitions and patterns of cognitions, either within single lists or across group members. This patterning is the focus of the next step in cognitive therapy. Once individuals are able to identify dysfunctional thoughts and feelings, they need to learn how to classify the thoughts into categories. Therapists need to decide when to initiate the process of categorizing thoughts. It is important not to confuse clients with the details of classification until the majority of group members have completed the identification process. For this reason, categorizing usually occurs during the next phase of therapy, when clients learn how to categorize and how to challenge their cognitions. Sometimes, however, some clients who have already mastered the tasks of identification will begin to see and inquire about patterns. Perhaps the best way to deal with these inquiries, if they are considered premature for the group, is for therapists to acknowledge that there are patterns, encourage individuals to look for patterns in their own thoughts, and explain that the investigation of these patterns represents the next step in therapy. Even though classification is not typically undertaken during the identification phase, therapists need to be aware of the different categories so that they can begin to assess the typical errors of each group member. Based on this preliminary assessment, leaders can decide what lecturettes to highlight, and in what order, during the change phase. In order to assist therapists in making their classification, we present here a system we found useful with older adults.

Classification systems may vary in breadth and inclusiveness, but fundamental to all is the recognition that (a) dysfunctional thoughts misrepresent the significance of past, present, or future events; (b) attributions or associations with good and bad events differ in object, intensity, and quality; and (c) self-other relationships are distorted by rules that are applied unequally.

In order to capture these various permutations of dysfunctional thoughts in a manner that will assist clients to use them for self-cueing and recall, the system of categorization must be reasonably comprehensive, simple, and believable. Such a system should balance the need for comprehensiveness with the desirability of limiting the categories to a number easily remembered by older individuals. The problem of memory is best addressed if one identifies the categories with memorable labels and cue words that are frequently present in the thoughts themselves. This approach is preferable to the use of abstract explanations, which are often forgotten.

It should be noted that we do not separately catalogue the general process of negative attribution. The tendency to perceive bad and good events as differing in stability (e.g., bad things last forever and good things are temporary), generalizability (e.g., bad things are more likely to occur than good things), and internal reference (e.g., bad things result from my acts while good things result from good fortune, fate, or others) is incorporated into our discussions of the various and more specific types of distortion. To this end, we typically identify seven categories of cognitive errors. We do not assume these categories are either mutually exclusive or exhaustive. They are, however, useful and generally comprehensible.

1. *Overgeneralization* is the most fundamental process in cognitive distortion. This process is inherent in virtually all recognizable patterns of dysfunctional thought. Thought can be overgeneralized with reference to time, situation, or person. We explain to clients that this fundamental error

of thinking is the tendency to equate one event (time or person) with all subsequent ones. Words that may cue clients to this pattern include *all, never,* and *always.*

2. *Awfulizing* is a label applied to a particular type of overgeneralization. In our categorization scheme, this term is applied to the tendency to exaggerate the negative aspects of present or anticipated events. Cueing words are those loaded with negative meaning that dramatize the power of these events. They include such words as *terrible, awful, devastating,* and *catastrophic.* Clients are typically asked to lend assistance in finding such words that characterize their own internal vocabularies.

3. *Self-expectations* represent exaggerated criteria of performance placed on oneself and usually are accompanied by such words as *have to, must, need to, can't, should,* and all of their derivatives. This cognitive error represents both a tendency to compare oneself to an overgeneralized, unrealistic view of others and a failure to generalize the weaknesses of others to oneself.

4. *Making demands on others* is a process closely related to placing unrealistic expectations on oneself. The critical differentiating feature is that the demand words (*have to, should,* etc.) are accompanied by pronouns such as *she, he, they,* and *you* rather than the personal *I.* Clients are taught to recognize these demand statements and the type of pronoun that accompanies them.

5. *Exaggerated self statements* bear a close resemblance to the foregoing patterns. For example, inherent in self-criticism is often the belief that one has or should have magical powers to predict or control others and events. Similarly, one exaggerates one's own importance by placing oneself in a category or under a demand that would be unrealistic for anyone else. The depressive belief that ''I am the biggest failure in the world,'' for example, masks the arrogance of the accompanying belief that ''I am one of a kind.'' We endeavor to teach clients to recognize these hidden but arrogant comparisons by sensitizing them to such cue words as *most, biggest, worst* and other superlatives and comparatives that they apply to themselves.

6. *Mindreading* is a label which we apply to the tendency to attribute negative, internal states to others. The pronoun *you* is targeted as the cue word in such statements and is followed by such additional cue words as *feel, think,* and *believe.* We teach clients that the cueing sentence is frequently completed with a comment that is either self defeating (e.g., ''You think that I'm a crackpot'') or accusatory (e.g., ''You think that golf is more important than I am'').

7. *Self-criticism* is the final category we typically describe for clients. This thought pattern is often applied in response to a mistake or unpredicted and negative outcome of behavior. Cue words are observed as global self-

attributions and frequently take the form of namecalling. Such cueing words as *bad, wimp, S.O.B.,* and *crazy* are frequently used, but clients are asked to supply their own "favorites" as well.

The classification of negative thoughts has several purposes. First, the categories serve clients as memory and recognition cues, so that an automatic thought can be more easily intercepted and challenged. For example, a client might experience a sense of panic and, after only a few seconds thought, be able to say "There I go, awfulizing again!" and institute a familiar and effective intervention for this kind of dysfunctional thought.

Perhaps, a more important reason for classifying negative cognitions is that each type or category of thought responds to a different kind of intervention. Many of the interventions overlap categories, but clients will be more effective in challenging their cognitions if they ask themselves the questions most appropriate for that category of error. For example, a client is sad because she thinks her new friend is bored with her. Another client blames himself because his daughter no longer practices her religion. In the first client's case, where the error is mindreading, it might be effective to ask what evidence the client has to support her belief that her friend is bored. In the second case, an error of self-criticism, it might be helpful to explore the extent to which any human being can be responsible for another's religious practice. Clearly, the approaches are different for the different types of errors and could not be interchanged with any effectiveness.

The third reason to classify thoughts concerns the identification of more generalized underlying assumptions and beliefs, which sometimes form a lifelong approach to living. Beck and his associates (1979) refer to these organizing beliefs as *schemas.* In the final weeks of therapy, should the group have advanced to this point, therapists can assist clients to identify their schemas, by exploring beliefs that underlie individual categories of thought. Although there are relatively few categories, the schemas themselves are highly idiosyncratic. There may, for example, be two people in the group who have unreasonably high self-expectations. The underlying schema, however, could be as different as "You can't get respect if you aren't better than everyone else" or "If you show weakness, people will destroy you" or "If I'm not perfect, God will not love me." Therapists will find the eventual task of identifying schemas easier if they have been alert from the start of the group to categories of cognitive error and generalized statements that could indicate underlying beliefs.

LECTURETTES

In our experience, short lecturettes are an effective way to communicate the basic principles of cognitive therapy. In this and the next two chapters, we present lecturettes we found appropriate to the phase in question.

Most aspects of cognitive therapy, from defining the concepts to implementing change techniques, have been included but, as with our discussion of the behavioral techniques, we have not attempted to provide an exhaustive list of topics. The reader is encouraged to read Beck et al. (1979) should further information be desired.

Therapists will add or delete topics for lecturettes according to the characteristics and needs of a particular group. For example, in a high-functioning group of older adults who are not severely depressed, it might be unnecessary to devote a lecturette to explain the relationship between pleasant activities and depression. A lecturette might be omitted because that particular dysfunctional thought does not arise for the people in the group or when the concept might require no formal explanation. Sometimes, a topic to which the therapists had intended to devote a lecturette arises in the course of an earlier group session and is endorsed by all group members as if it were common knowledge, thus making the proposed lecturette unnecessary. It is also possible that, for example, not a single member of the group shows any evidence of a particular type of erroneous thinking. The therapists might well decide in this case that a lecturette on that topic would be irrelevant and would not justify the time involved.

For the sake of consistency, we developed a format according to which all lecturettes could be written. Our examples of completed lecturettes employ this format, but rigid adherence to this outline is neither necessary nor recommended. The most important aspects of any lecturette, regardless of format, are that (a) the presentation be as clear as possible, so that the main point of the lecturette is not obscured, and (b) the examples used are appropriate for the population. The effect is more powerful if the therapists can use actual situations from the lives of the members as examples. It is also important (c) that therapists assure themselves that members have understood the topic and can apply it to their own situations through homework assignments based on the lecturette. Just as the lecturettes themselves will be altered to suit the needs of the group, so too the homework assignments will, in all likelihood, require adjustment to the functioning level and progress of individual group members.

In the collaboration/identification phase, most of the lecturettes pertain to behavioral techniques. The one specifically cognitive lecturette, on the relationship between thoughts and feelings, is central to therapy. It may be necessary to present this concept in several different ways, as separate lecturettes, in order to ensure that clients understand the concept.

Suggested Outline for Lecturettes

1. *Explanation*. The main point of the lecturette is explained. Illustrative examples are written on the board in the familiar two- or three-column style. In order to check comprehension, members are asked to further

explain the examples or to apply the concept to new examples supplied by the leader. When necessary (if, for example, the discussion has wandered away from the lecturette), leaders will summarize the main point before moving on.
2. *Personal application.* In this section, members supply examples appropriate to the lecturette from their own experience. Several of these might be analyzed on the board.
3. *Homework.* Leaders outline an assignment based on the lecturette, providing a rationale, if necessary. There might be several levels of homework if leaders judge it best that different group members be assigned tasks of different complexity. Leaders always make certain that group members understand and are willing to attempt the assignment.

Examples

Relationship Between Thoughts and Feelings. Before beginning this lecturette, write the following on the board:

Situation	Thoughts	Feelings
Letter from son		Mother:
		Father:

Explanation: Many people believe that feelings, such as joy, sadness, anger, etc., are caused by other people's behavior or by things that happen to us; therefore, we assume that we have no control over our feelings. In reality, our feelings are caused by the thoughts and beliefs we have learned to have about an event or about someone's behavior.

For example, a mother and father receive a letter from their son, from whom they have not heard in many years. Mother cries tears of joy, but father's reaction is intense anger. Since they are both reading the same letter, the letter itself cannot be responsible for these very different reactions. (Under *Feelings* on the board, add "joy" and "anger"). When the mother reads the letter, she thinks "Thank God he's alive," and she is happy. When father reads it, he thinks "How dare he worry us by not writing earlier!" and he is angry. (On the board, fill in the designated thoughts for mother and father).

Thus, the way each parent thought about the letter was responsible for their emotions. The letter did not cause the feelings.

For a second example, Mrs. Smith's physician tells her that her blood pressure is still high, but did not increase in the last month. (On the board write, "BP high" under *Situation* and "Depressed, anxious," and "Hopeful" under *Feelings*.)

If Mrs. Smith thinks, "It's no better! I'm never going to get better!" she will feel depressed and anxious. If she thinks, "At least it's no worse. Maybe it's on the mend," she will feel somewhat hopeful. Thus, the blood pressure level itself doesn't make her feel a certain way, but rather the way she thinks about what the doctor has told her. (On the board, complete her thoughts.)

Consider another example. Imagine that you are alone in the house at night when you hear a strange noise in the kitchen. (On board write, "Noise in kitchen" under *Situation* and "Scared" and "Reassured" under *Feelings*.)

What thoughts would make you feel scared? (Fill this in.) What would you have to think in order to feel reassured? (Fill this in.)

Personal application: Can anyone think of a recent situation where you felt sad, angry, depressed, etc.? Is there a situation that occurs often in your life, where you feel bad? (Elicit several examples and write them on the board, fill in the Situation and Feelings columns. Elicit from each volunteer the thoughts that contributed to the feelings. If this is difficult, ask the volunteer or other group members to invent or imagine what thoughts might have occurred.)

Suppose you wanted to feel differently, what might a more comfortable or less distressing feeling be in this situation? (Write them on the board.)

Has anyone had an experience of first feeling bad about a situation, then feeling somewhat better? (Write the situation and both sets of feelings on board. Elicit both sets of thoughts.)

Homework: Often, feelings are very strong and occur so rapidly that it's hard to believe any thoughts are involved. Especially when we are in the habit of experiencing a particular feeling quite often, the thoughts that precede the feeling become automatic, so that we do not think them consciously. Before we can do anything to change these thoughts, we have to learn to "catch" them. Before we can catch thoughts, we must notice when unpleasant feelings happen, since they are the clue to what we are thinking.

If this lecturette is presented early in the phase, homework will consist of asking clients to complete only two columns, Situation and Feelings. Ask members to gather several examples during the week, focusing primarily on unpleasant feelings.

If clients are already accomplished in two-column records, ask them to complete the Thought column. Emphasize that this may be difficult and, if they cannot do it, they should at least complete the Situation and Feelings columns. They will be helped in group next week to identify their thoughts. More advanced members might be asked to include examples of occasions where their thoughts, and consequently their feelings, about a situation, changed.

Relationship Between Depression and Pleasant Activities. Explanation: Depressed people have little energy or motivation to perform many of their normal activities. They even stop doing things that used to give them pleasure. Soon, they are doing very little that is pleasurable and, so, feel even more depressed. They then feel like doing even less, and the situation gets worse. Because they have no energy, they tend to wait for others to plan activities for them instead of planning for themselves. For example, Joe used to be a keen gardener. He derived several different types of pleasure from his garden: he enjoyed the look of it; he enjoyed the feeling of accomplishment; he liked the praise he got from others; he liked the taste of the fresh vegetables; he liked the money he saved; he also liked feeling healthy after his work outdoors. When he became depressed, he felt too tired to tend the garden, and the more neglected it got, the less he felt able to tackle it. Eventually, he stopped going into the garden at all, not realizing how much pleasure he was really losing.

In another example, a woman used to enjoy serving coffee after church services each Sunday. She also liked reading mystery novels, and used to write long letters to friends of many years standing. When she became depressed, she felt too self-conscious to serve coffee, she found it hard to concentrate on her books, and she couldn't think of anything cheerful to say in her letters. Gradually, she stopped all of these pleasurable activities, and the less she did, the more it seemed like a chore to get back into them. With less and less pleasure in her life, she became more and more depressed. Her husband tried to cheer her up by taking her for car rides or out to eat, but these weren't any fun either, and she felt guilty for not appreciating his efforts.

So we can see that depression takes the pleasure out of life, and as we stop doing anything that could be pleasant, we get more depressed.

Personal application: What activities did you used to enjoy that would still be possible for you, but that you have given up since you became depressed? What excuses do you give for not doing them any more? (Explain that the loss of pleasure and the lack of energy are symptoms of depression—"that's your depression talking.") Which two or three of these activities would take the least effort (especially in terms of time, money, preparation, energy, etc.) to pick up again?

Homework: In order to reverse the downward spiral, depressed people have to start being active again, doing things they used to enjoy, even if they do not enjoy them as much now as they once did, otherwise they get more and more inactive and depressed. They have to do these for themselves instead of waiting for others to help them or to suggest activities. Choose one or two small, easy activities that you used to enjoy and that you could do at least once this week. Decide when you will do them, at a time when you are not too tired, and for how long. Other people may be involved, but you should be in charge of the activity. Make a note of your feelings both before and after the activity, and bring this information to the next meeting.

Note: If you think it is selfish to plan your own pleasure, consider that this is your effort to overcome depression, which will bring pleasure to others who are concerned about you and don't want you to be depressed.

Note: Because of your depression you should not expect to enjoy the activities very much, not as much as you used to. That is normal and will change as you keep practicing. It takes time to learn again how to enjoy yourself. The important points about this homework are that you get started somewhere and that you pay attention to even the smallest bit of pleasure you can find in the activity. Perhaps your main pleasure this time will be that you made the effort to do something.

The following possible topics for lecturettes could be developed as above, or in any way that seems appropriate to communicate the material.

Relationship Between Mastery Activities and Depression. A frequent feature of depression is the conviction of inadequacy, which results partly from the reduced ability to concentrate, the retardation of speech and movement, and invidious comparisons with one's own previous performance. As a sense of mastery decreases, so does involvement in activities that could provide a sense of mastery. At the same time, the self-blame, the self-expectations, and the depression increase.

Scheduling Activities. The anhedonia and inertia of depression lead to low levels of activity and, frequently, the failure to complete tasks. These, in turn, give rise to self-blame for laziness, boredom, and the belief that one is no longer capable of doing anything at all. Scheduling activities restores structure and a sense of self-control; it acts as a stimulus to perform preplanned activities and provides evidence of achievement. A structured day tends to pass more quickly and be somewhat less boring than a day without plans.

Social Activities. When depressed people withdraw from contact with others they lose both a source of pleasure and stimulation and the opportunity to practice and maintain social skills. As withdrawal increases, they become correspondingly less confident in social situations, and tend to withdraw further. Prolonged loss of contact frequently results in the loss of friendships and a reduction in one's social circle that persists after the depression has lifted. Depressed people need to begin to reverse the spiral by increasing their social contacts in small steps.

INITIATION OF
BEHAVIORAL CHANGE

In older adults, both age and circumstances tend to mitigate against high levels of physical or social involvement and activity. These activities are reduced even further by depression. When clients are severely depressed, cognitive therapy may be impossible until they are restored to a level of physical functioning consistent with their physical abilities; even mildly depressed older clients may need more assistance than younger people in overcoming the inertia of depression. In the identification/collaboration phase, therefore, it is often advisable to introduce techniques that reinforce behavioral/social activity, in order to help clients participate fully in the cognitive therapeutic process.

Many negative beliefs in depressed clients center around performance ability, self-management, and control of symptoms. These are precisely the areas targeted by behavioral techniques and, thus, behavioral assignments serve a dual purpose within cognitive therapy. The techniques themselves provide a way to test clients' beliefs about their ability to function and to overcome depression. Conversely, changing those cognitions that impede performance of the techniques improves performance. Thus, cognitive and behavioral techniques fit well together and enhance each other's effectiveness.

Reinforcement techniques are especially advantageous at this stage. Reinforcement has a beneficial effect on clients' motivation for therapy, and when the techniques are tailored to individual needs, they result in small but tangible gains that restore a sense of power and hope to clients. Within a group, this effect is enhanced, since clients act as positive role models for each other, and members have ample opportunity to both give and receive positive reinforcement for their efforts. In addition, the use of reinforcement techniques allows clients to become accustomed to the practice of focusing on relevant in vivo behavior changes, rather than on the common depressive ruminations over past and present miseries.

Behavioral homework assignments also can be valuable in generating cognitions that provide rich individualized material for cognitive appraisal and treatment. For example, a client who successfully completes "activity scheduling" can be led to correct the cognition "I can't do anything anymore" when confronted with the inaccuracy of this belief. The client's completion of the assignment furnishes clear proof to refute the belief. Even when a particular assignment is not completed to the satisfaction of the client, the dysfunctional cognitions that arise as a result of this apparent "failure" can be examined during the next session. Such thoughts as "If I can't do it as well as I would have done it when I was younger, then it's not worth my even trying" or "I don't fit into this group because

I can't even do the simplest task" are likely to strike sympathetic chords in other groups members and often allow therapists and members to provide encouragement for a second effort. Should they persist, these cognitions can be used as examples of dysfunctional thoughts and approached within a cognitive framework (as illustrated in Table 5.3).

Behavioral assignments may require some modification for use with depressed older adults, in order to increase compliance. Out of disgust with what they view as their inadequacy, and out of an inability to assess how far their energy will stretch, older clients often overestimate the amount they can achieve. When they fall short of their expectations they feel guilty, discouraged, and helpless, and they lose much of their motivation to continue. Changes in perceptual and attentional processes and in physical capacity can also affect both understanding and performance of behavioral assignments, with consequent loss of motivation to proceed.

It is important that behavioral homework be engineered to maximize the potential for success. This can be achieved in several ways. Therapists should ensure that clients set personally realistic and attainable goals with additional long-term, stepwise objectives. It is preferable that a client reach only the first step of an assignment with some success than attempt and fail to reach a second or third step. Since it is likely that group members will be at different levels of functioning, and in different life circumstances, many homework and behavioral assignments will need to be adapted to the capability of each person. Unfortunately, the ability of some members to perform more complex or extended tasks than others can give rise to comparisons, accompanied by such negative cognitions as "This just proves I'm no good" and "I should be able to keep up with everyone else." These cognitions need to be addressed within a cognitive therapy

Table 5.3. Cognitive Approach to Uncompleted Homework

A Situation	B Thoughts	C Feelings
Uncompleted homework	If I can't do something well it is not worth trying.	Helpless, inadequate
	I don't belong in this group. I'm slower than the rest.	Alone, inadequate

Underlying Belief
Some criterion of performance for the individual is expected by self or others for one's effort to be of value.

Interventions
1. "Does the effort count for anything?"
2. "How is success or failure determined?"
3. "Does one failure mean success is not possible?"

framework, which at this stage will consist largely of helping clients to redefine "success" as effort rather than total and complete achievement. Clients are also encouraged to adopt the belief that any progress, however slight, is positive and valuable and constitutes proof that they are overcoming depression. It is frequently helpful to explain the effect of depression on concentration and energy and the consequent need for clients to lower their expectations of themselves, at least temporarily. They can be encouraged in their hope that, as depression lifts, their performance will increase. This attitude of self-nurturance can be effective in increasing both relaxation and efforts to complete assignments.

The behavioral techniques described below are not intended to be exhaustive, but are those that have typically had success in promoting initial behavioral change in depressed clients.

Activity Scheduling

A reduction in purposeful and pleasurable daily activity is almost inevitable in both retarded and agitated depression and makes an appropriate target for initial behavioral intervention. In these preliminary stages, clients are asked to schedule a variety of activities for the week ahead, attempt to keep the schedule, and record their success.

Purpose and Benefits. Both social and physical activity present problems for the typical depressed client. As the symptoms of depression (confusion, loss of energy, lack of interest, etc.) set in, clients tend to take longer to complete tasks, perform them with less satisfaction, feel overwhelmed and incompetent, and become convinced that their efforts are bound to fail. In social situations, they often feel irritable and critical toward others and believe that they are disliked and represent nothing but a burden to others. Experiences and beliefs such as these result in withdrawal from many or all daily activities, including contact with others—a withdrawal that, in turn, can initiate self-criticism and intensify the belief that they are helpless to cope with even the simplest task. Not surprisingly, these negative attitudes and isolating behaviors are often inconvenient and irritating to spouses, family, and friends, who are unable to entirely conceal their impatience. Unfortunately, the kindly efforts to plan interesting activities for the clients by significant others only reinforce the depressive cognitions and can actually increase inactivity. Older adults, who might already have lost considerable autonomy, can ill afford the dependency that can accompany a failure to eat, to groom themselves, to pay bills, etc. When the lethargy extends to lack of compliance with medication schedules, it can be dangerous to one's health.

Activity scheduling, therefore, has several purposes. Probably, the most important of these is to reverse the downward spiral of helplessness, inactivity, and depression. A second purpose is to counteract, by means of concrete proof of activity, the client's exaggerated belief that he or she "never accomplishes anything" or has lost the capacity to cope. Also valuable is the contribution of the activity schedule to the client's sense of self-management, of being in control of at least certain segments of life. The visible increase in activity level also convinces others that the client is still capable and independent.

Initially, the technique can serve an assessment function, as it demonstrates the extent of the client's withdrawal from or difficulties with minor daily activities. The way in which the assignment is completed also indicates the client's ability to plan ahead and to perform self-management tasks. Later on in therapy, the early schedules of activity can be used to demonstrate to the client how much progress has been made.

Procedure. The following steps are used to initiate activity scheduling.

1. A rationale for the technique is provided to clients, including the following points: (a) Three major symptoms of depression are fatigue, loss of interest, and difficulty in starting and finishing tasks; (b) Because tasks are more difficult and less rewarding, depressed people tend to procrastinate or avoid daily activities, even those they used to enjoy or do well. This procrastination and avoidance applies to social relationships as well as to intrapersonal activities; (c) Inactivity can produce harmful effects on health, on relationships, on self-esteem; (d) The situation gets worse as withdrawal increases. A good way to reverse the process is to deliberately engage in selected activities on a daily basis.
2. Negative thoughts are elicited from the group members about their decreased functioning and the resultant emotions.
3. Clients are then provided with a blank schedule for the daytime hours of the coming week and asked to insert one item in each hour's space. They are also guided through an average day, writing in all activities that are part of their normal routine. Thus, they are asked to include meals, baths, household chores, reading the newspaper, phone calls, etc.
4. Clients are then asked to fill in the remaining spaces. Frequently, depressed clients find one part of the day more difficult than others, usually the "dead" afternoon hours or the evening time before bed. By sharing their own time use and by using their imaginations and knowledge of each other, group members can be helpful in providing ideas for activities.
5. When schedules are completed (at least in part), clients will be asked

to perform at least a part of each activity as scheduled during the coming week and to check off each time an effort is made. It is important to emphasize that performing the activity at the correct time is what counts initially, not how well it was done or for how long. For example, if reading the paper is the task planned for Monday between 2 and 3 P.M., then it is enough to pick up the paper and read only the headlines. It does not matter if the person cannot concentrate or falls asleep after 10 minutes.

6. Clients are asked to bring the schedule with them to the next session, regardless of whether they have been able to follow it completely.

7. An effort is made to put homework in a framework that will be likely to increase compliance. For example, therapists might ask clients to compare themselves to a man with a broken leg, whose cast has just been removed. Obviously, he must exercise or the leg will stay weak. It is equally obvious that exercising will be painful for a while, and he will not run marathons for some time. The man will also most probably feel discouraged and find it hard to believe that just walking round the yard is of any use at all. But if he does not start somewhere, the leg may be permanently damaged. Since most elderly people are also parents, this particular metaphor can be effective if they are asked to imagine that the injured person is a child. What would they say to that child in order to persuade him or her to exercise despite the pain and the minimal progress?

If clients remain skeptical about the value of the exercise, it might be suggested that they perform an experiment in which they take careful note of and compare their feelings during times when they are doing nothing (which usually means brooding) and at times when they are active. The results can then be discussed the following week.

Discussion. Despite, or perhaps because of, its simplicity, Activity Scheduling can be problematic in several ways. Sometimes clients fail to understand the purpose and assume that the therapist is requiring hourly accomplishments they feel they have no energy or motivation to perform. For these clients, it might be helpful to emphasize once more the enervating and demoralizing effects of depression and the step-by-step nature of recovery. If possible, mobilize other group members to help persuade reluctant clients to define the least amount of acceptable effort.

Other clients can have the unrealistic expectation that simply following the schedule will significantly reduce their symptoms and are disappointed when this does not occur. This concern should be anticipated by explaining that during recovery from depression, improved functioning frequently precedes symptomatic relief. In the meantime, they need to focus on how successful they are being in taking control of their lives again.

Some clients might wish to fill their schedules with all the tasks they have neglected for months, without considering whether this is realistic. The therapist should encourage clients to write down only those activities within their resources of time and energy, so as to avoid exhaustion at best and a sense of failure at worst.

A practical consideration in using this technique in a group setting is the amount of time that can be required to complete a full week's schedule, especially if the whole group gets involved in the process for each member. One way to handle this potential time problem is to ask clients to bring to the session a schedule showing the previous week's activities; this schedule can be used as a model for planning a week ahead. Alternatively, therapists might plan only one or two days of the following week during the session and either ask clients to follow the schedule for those days only or ask them to complete the schedule at home.

By following the daily schedule, the client is usually able to cope with small but necessary tasks, such as bill paying, that have been a source of procrastination and worry up to this point. The resulting sense of accomplishment can reassure the client that recovery from depression is possible.

Mastery Technique

The mastery technique follows naturally on the technique of activity scheduling. When the group members have been accustomed to scheduling and completing an increased number of activities of any kind, it is time for them to plan specific activities that will provide a sense of accomplishment rather than simply fill in time. In addition to noting whether or not an activity was attempted, group members are usually asked to rate selected items for a sense of mastery or achievement and the impact of the activity or mood.

Purpose and Benefits. Typically, depressed clients make three errors with respect to mastery. First, they tend to underestimate or denigrate the amount they are, in fact, accomplishing, seeing only the tasks left unfinished or the long list of jobs not yet started. Second, they have unrealistic expectations of how much they should be able to accomplish, comparing themselves to others whom they view as more productive and to themselves in predepression days. This particular comparison can be very upsetting when increased age or poor health is responsible for part of the deterioration. In these cases, clients' beliefs that they are not as productive as before are grounded in reality but the devastating impact of being unproductive results from the negative schema of their depression. The third error, typical of the catastrophizing that occurs in depression, is that these clients view their lack of mastery as proof that they have ceased to be competent human beings and are on the way to complete loss of autonomy, ending in placement in a nursing home or other care center. Inevitably, someone in the group will raise the fear of the much-publicized Alzheimer's disease. The purpose of the mastery exercise, then, is to assist clients to set realistic goals, make an accurate appraisal of their accomplishments, and prove to themselves and not coincidentally to their families, that they can still function well enough to remain in control of their lives.

Procedure. The steps in implementing mastery exercises are as follows:

1. Clients are provided with a rationale for mastery techniques that includes these points: (a) A sense of accomplishment, the ability to meet commitments, and manage one's own life are important components of both cognitive and affective self-esteem; (b) The ability to cope with even simple everyday tasks is strongly affected by each symptom of depression, such as fatigue, lack of concentration, and feeling overwhelmed. It is not weakness of will; (c) Because of their depression, clients cannot be expected to perform at predepression levels. The building process needs to be gradual and any signs of progress, however minimal, should be interpreted as success.
2. Each client is asked to choose one or two simple tasks that are of some importance and that could reasonably be completed or well started before the next group session. These tasks must be within the client's resources of time, energy, money, support, supplies, etc., and must be something the client can take pride in doing.
3. The client might then be asked to write each task or activity into the week's schedule choosing a time most likely to be conducive to success; e.g., when the client's pain is least, when energy is highest, when the day has not been too stressful, when the client is not too heavily medicated.
4. The therapist then might define mastery, referring to concepts discussed in the rationale, and explain how to rate mastery, using a method that is acceptable to the group (e.g., 1=I got started; 2=I finished about half of the task; 3=I completed what I had planned).
5. Each client is asked to tell the group what he or she has planned, to convince the group that the tasks are feasible, and to set a mastery level that seems reasonable. The group members and the therapist then help the client to adjust the task difficulty or the mastery level, if it seems that such adjustment would increase the probability of success.

Discussion. The main objectives of using mastery techniques are to help clients set realistic goals and evaluate their success positively. If clients can think only of complex projects, it will probably be necessary to use a "graded task assignment" technique (to be discussed next). One of the more difficult attitudes to address when using the mastery technique is clients' impatience with the progress of their own accomplishments and with the therapy itself. Such beliefs as "This shouldn't be taking so long; I should be better by now," "This therapy is going nowhere," and "What's the use of a life where your biggest achievement is balancing a checkbook?" can sabotage the effective use of the mastery techniques. Despite their impatience, however, clients should be encouraged to set low standards for success, especially if they are severely depressed and have accomplished little for a considerable time. Some clients, particularly ones who have few possessions and who live alone in impoverished surroundings, may be unable to think of tasks they would like to accomplish. Other group members are usually able to help such clients discover one or two meaningful changes they would like to make.

Graded Task Assignment

Graded task assignment is a technique in which the client performs specific tasks or activities arranged in a hierarchy of difficulty. As competence increases, the person proceeds from relatively simple to more complex tasks. These graded tasks can be a series of related activities or one complex project divided into small steps or parts.

Purpose and Benefits. Graded tasks can be a necessary adjunct to mastery techniques. With clients who have very low levels of functioning, who report becoming confused by complex tasks, or who feel a need to undertake longer and more complicated projects, it will usually be advantageous to divide the major task into several minor ones. As well as low energy levels, depressed people often lack confidence in their ability to see a project through; even if they start a difficult chore they tend to give up easily, quitting the activity at the first sign of difficulty.

Older adults must often contend with several additional problems: the reduced energy levels and health difficulties so often attendant to aging can make once simple tasks far more threatening, even for those who are not depressed; new circumstances, such as widowhood or a sudden change in financial status, can provide challenges in the form of completely unfamiliar tasks. Especially among couples who have held to traditional roles, it can be overwhelming to a man to have to learn to cook for himself or to a woman to have to manage money. When it is a case of learning new tasks, the most efficient way for anyone, depressed or not, is usually to follow a graded task method.

Although depressed persons may have valid reasons to feel as if they can do nothing at all, in truth they can function, although doing so is likely to be more difficult than it was in the past. The main purpose of graded task assignments is to help clients recognize this truth. As they experience success in reaching specific objectives, and receive reinforcement from the therapists and other group members for this success, they begin to recognize that they are capable of learning new skills and functioning at or close to predepression levels.

Procedure. The implementation of graded tasks employs the following steps:

1. A rationale for the technique is provided including (a) Examples and explanations of how to break a task into steps and to arrange these steps in either a time sequence or a hierarchy of difficulty. For example, the goal of preparing an income tax return can be broken down into many steps from putting the checks and receipts together in one spot to filling out the form. Similarly, cleaning out the possessions of one's husband or learning to cook a meal can be broken down into step-by-step activities. (b) It should be emphasized that it is easier to complete one step than to face the whole task. People not only feel less overwhelmed but tend to do a more thorough job when the task is short and simple. (c) Clients are frequently reminded that fatigue and depression are related and that it is advantageous to avoid making too many demands of oneself when tired.
2. The therapist identifies a project with each client, which he or she would like to complete but feels is too large to handle at this point.
3. Reactions that a client might have to beginning the project should be discussed, including the fear of being unable to complete the project.
4. Tasks should be apportioned into small steps, arranged in a hierarchy of difficulty, the first task being a relatively easy one that the client is likely to complete.
5. The therapist should be sensitive in initiating a discussion with group members of ways in which they can arrange to make the task as pleasant and easy as possible, such as asking for help, getting advice, listening to favorite music while working.
6. After each attempt, and before moving to the next step in the hierarchy, the therapist should evaluate with the client how the effort went. Typically, this discussion has three parts. The first and most important is to listen to the client's initial evaluation of the performance, even if it belittles the achievement. The second step is to encourage a more realistic evaluation of the performance, and the third is to note that the client reached the goal through his or her own efforts and, thus, is regaining self-control.

Discussion. The therapist might encounter difficulty in using graded task assignments at a few points. Recall that the purpose of the assignment is to show the client that he or she is capable of performing. It is, therefore, essential that the client recognize success as success. The therapist must discuss the accomplishment long enough with the client to get past the inevitable disclaimers and comparisons ("It wasn't as good, long, fast, straight, tasty, etc. as I used to do it." "My brother, friend, neighbor, spouse, etc., could do it twice as well.") until the point is reached where the client acknowledges that he or she did achieve something, however small, and that this constitutes valid evidence that he or she is not incapable of being productive.

The client who fails, especially at one of the early tasks on the hierarchy, is likely to take this failure as evidence that his or her belief is correct: "I really can't do anything." If it looks as if there is a good chance of failure, the client should be persuaded to begin the hierarchy at a lower level and reduce the size of the steps. This strategy is especially appropriate when the client is attempting to learn a new task.

When discussing each task with the client, therapists should try to get the client to evaluate the accomplishment positively, although care should be taken not to exaggerate its value. To be functioning at such a low level and taking such small steps can be embarrassing to many people and the therapist's enthusiasm might add to this embarrassment. It should be acknowledged, therefore, that the task itself may not be impressive, but the effort is significant because of its implications for future progress.

Pleasure Technique

One of the most unpleasant aspects of depression is the persistent and pervasive lack of enjoyment. Pleasure techniques help clients begin relearning how to enjoy life, by engaging in activities that have the potential to provide pleasure and by rating the pleasure they feel, as a way to focus on the positive rather than on the negative aspects.

Purpose and Benefits. As depression sets in, clients typically withdraw from activities that no longer give them pleasure; at the same time, they belittle any small amount of enjoyment they still derive ("I only enjoyed it for an hour," "It was okay but my back hurt"). Thus, the loss of pleasure is vulnerable to distortion and exaggeration. The situation is complicated for older adults by the changes in physical strength, in living circumstances, or in available companionship that make it impossible to engage in formerly enjoyable activities. In depressed people, this reality can lead readily to several distorted beliefs: that they are losing everything pleasurable in life, that prospects for the future are grim, that life is so boring and miserable, and death is certainly no more than a few months or years away.

The purpose of planning and rating pleasant activities is, therefore, twofold. Gradually, the client relearns how to have fun and how to focus on, and be satisfied with, the pleasurable highlights of an activity, rather than expecting a whole event to be exciting. This positively affects the belief that life is still worth living. A second purpose is to increase the menu of available pleasant activities, particularly for those who have lost former pleasures. The realization that there are new areas for enjoyment can be a powerful motive for resuming a full, active life.

Procedure. The steps for implementing pleasure techniques include:

1. Providing a rationale for pleasure techniques, making the following points: (a) In depression, there is a downward spiral of reduced pleasure, reduced participation in pleasant activity, and reduced pleasure, with accompanying cognitions about life being boring or not worth living. (b) The number and type of available pleasurable activities often changes as people age; it is therefore important to seek new ways to enjoy oneself. (c) Engaging in pleasant activities tends to decrease depression. (d) Depressed people lose the habit of enjoying themselves and need to relearn it. At first, they should expect low levels of pleasure that may last for only a short time.
2. Clients are next asked to identify one or two activities that used to give them pleasure and that are readily accessible now, without too great an expenditure of time or energy.
3. Clients are shown how to enter these activities into their weekly schedules choosing times that will be most conducive to success.
4. Each member is then asked to tell the group what he or she has planned. With the help of group members, therapists elicit from each client what is expected to be enjoyable about each activity.
5. The therapists then help the group to decide on a rating scale for pleasure (e.g., 1 = a very small amount of pleasure; 2 = noticeable pleasure; 3 = more pleasure than I expected). The therapists should remind the group at this point that they are not allowed to use negative ratings such as "Not as much as I used to enjoy it."

Discussion. In using the pleasure technique, the most frequent complaint is from clients who claim that nothing gives them any pleasure at all, so "what's the point?" These clients can be asked to engage in formerly enjoyable activities, not with any expectations of pleasure, but simply in order to evaluate these activities and to get back into the habit of deliberately pursuing the possibility of pleasure. They can be assured that pleasure will come later.

Sometimes clients cannot think of a pleasurable activity, perhaps because of drastic lifestyle changes, as for example a person who has recently become blind or a client who clings to the belief that only large pleasures count. The group can be especially helpful with such people, either by encouraging them to build a new repertoire of pleasant activities or by sharing some of their own small experiences that give pleasure. Incidentally, in convincing others that enjoyment is still possible, clients usually convince themselves to some extent, consequently approaching the assignment, themselves, with greater enthusiasm.

Chapter 6
Phase Three:
Cognitive Change

The purpose of the cognitive change phase is to move clients from the process of identifying dysfunctional thoughts to the process of changing these thoughts in a manner likely to alleviate depression. To this end, the objectives of the change phase are to teach clients how and when to question the validity of their thoughts, to implement alternative thinking processes, and to practice such alternatives through homework assignments and other outside activities. The general format of the sessions remains the same as during the identification phase of treatment; the differences are in the emphasis placed on change in the lecturettes and in the greater time alloted for one-to-one contact work.

The change phase often overlaps the identification/collaboration phase, usually beginning about the fifth or sixth week of therapy. The initiation of this stage is determined by the clinician's sense that collaboration has been achieved within the group and that clients are adequately familiar with the nature of dysfunctional thoughts, in general, and with those particular dysfunctional thoughts that characterize their own depression. Since different individuals might be ready to move on at different times, the clinician's judgment of each client's readiness to implement individualized treatment interventions becomes critical for maintaining a collaborative spirit among group members. Clients can be considered to have adequately mastered the tasks of phase two when they have developed a list of their negative cognitions and demonstrated the ability to monitor these thoughts via homework assignments. This list will serve both as a source of targets for change in phase three and a means by which clients can evaluate their gains in phase four. For those individuals who still appear to have difficulty in identifying or monitoring thoughts, it is appropriate to focus on behavioral techniques during the change phase, allowing these techniques and the positive support of the group to carry the burden of invoking change in depressive symptoms.

A feature of cognitive therapy that accommodates individual differences is large amounts of therapy accomplished through one-to-one interactions (contact work). These interactions allow the therapist to begin moving different clients into the change phase at different points. By also individualizing homework assignments and remaining sensitive to each client's particular struggles, therapists can ease the transition between phases. Indeed, as some clients begin working on change activities, they provide motivation and even modeling for other clients who lag behind somewhat. As a cardinal principle, however, one does not encourage or define cognitive change for specific clients until they have clearly established the ability both to identify important cognitive patterns in their own experience and to appreciate the impact of these cognitions on their mood.

The possibility of change lies in the client's ability to successfully eradicate cognitive errors. This process is facilitated by the use of questions designed to challenge specific erroneous concepts. A classification system for identifying the major errors in thinking was presented in Chapter 5 in order to enable therapists to tailor change activities as closely as possible to the cognitive errors of the group. Table 6.1 presents these errors as they might occur in reaction to a sample situation, together with examples of questions therapists can use to challenge each view of the situation and to evoke change.

The list presented in Table 6.1 does not, of course, exhaust the questions the therapist might use; with practice, therapists become adept at creating a variety of questions that can help clients explore, assess, and understand their errors in thinking. Therapists' ability to use questions rather than statements or other persuasion is critical, since it is important that clients reach conclusions about their cognitive errors for themselves rather than be coerced into accepting the therapist's view. New viewpoints and beliefs that clients develop under the guidance of therapeutic questioning carry more conviction and are more likely to persist over time than those imposed by a therapist to whom clients merely acquiesce.

Restructuring cognitions through questioning is assisted by an extension of the three-column record technique learned in the identification/collaboration phase. In the change phase, clients learn to add a fourth column in order to identify possible alternative thoughts. For example, a client, John, went shopping prior to the group meeting and found, when he came to pay for his purchases, that he had forgotten his wallet. He concluded that, because he had been forgetful, he was getting senile and consequently became frightened. John recorded the facts of the situation, his thoughts and his feelings in three columns and was then instructed on how to add a fourth column. In the fourth column, he recorded alternative thoughts to those that had caused him to become frightened, such as

Table 6.1. Cognitive Errors and Therapeutic Questions

Situation: Yesterday when I walked into the dining room, three women whom I know very well were already seated at a table in the middle of the room eating their lunch. They did not invite me to join them or even say hello to me. I was so upset that I went back to my room without eating.

Cognitive Error	Self Statement	Therapeutic Question
Overgeneralization (If it's true once it's true always, for all people.)	I guess my friends are all deserting me.	Is there an exception to your belief?
Awfulizing (Anything bad that happens is a catastrophe.)	It was devastating. I felt so hurt. It ruined my whole week.	How much importance do you want this one incident to have in your life?
Unrealistic Expectations of Self	I should have been able to control myself and act with dignity.	Is your standard too high? What can you reasonably expect?
Demands on Others	They shouldn't treat me like that. They should have invited me to join them.	Is your standard too high? What can you reasonably expect?
Exaggerating Self-Importance	Everyone noticed how they humiliated me.	What's your evidence that everybody noticed you?
Mind Reading	They were thinking I'm not good enough to be their friend.	What's your evidence? Is there any other way to explain their behavior?
Self-Blame	I must have offended them in some way.	How much are you really to blame for their behavior?

See lecturettes on pp. 82–94 for further explanation of Table 6.1.

"Everyone forgets things on occasion," "Forgetting my wallet doesn't have to mean that I'm going senile at all." John's fourth column record is illustrated in Table 6.2, together with other examples.

Categorizing cognitive errors, challenging them, and developing new methods of thinking can be facilitated by three fundamental, therapeutic methodologies. The first method is familiar to clients from phase two, through concepts presented in lecturettes and subsequently applied to homework assignments. The second method of approaching the issue of change is by means of individual contact work. The third method is to employ behavioral strategies to enhance activity levels and alter interpersonal environments.

LECTURETTES

As in phase two, lecturettes are used to introduce topics of importance and provide the basic foundation of knowledge from which to implement change. One should not assume that lecturettes produce change, in their own right, however. We adhere to the assumption that the most influential changes accrue with active self-discovery. Individual contact work and behavioral techniques facilitate such involvement. However, certain concepts require a base of information before the client can obtain maximal benefit from this individualized work. Lecturettes serve this purpose.

In the third phase of treatment, the lecturettes have two objectives: discussing the nature of a specific cognitive error and explaining how to challenge it. Homework proceeding from lecturettes is, therefore, presented in two parts: one relating to identification of the error and the other to countering that error. In some groups, it is possible to expect clients to attempt both parts of the homework after the initial presentation of the lecturette. Usually, it is most effective to assign the identification homework one week, discuss the resulting examples and practice challenging them during the next session, and only then assign the second part of the homework. As usual, therapists will decide how fast to proceed with lecturette material according to the ease with which members understand and apply the concepts. The following examples outline our methods of presenting key concepts of distorted thoughts and can be modified to accommodate the foregoing concerns.

Overgeneralization

Explanation. Depressed people tend to see a single incident as a sign that a great deal more is wrong. If one flower fails to bloom in the garden, this seems proof that nothing will bloom and that the person is a terrible gardener. This form of cognitive error, called *overgeneralization*, is responsible for much depression, because it paints the whole world black. For example, a man uses a new type of latch to fix his gate and puts it on wrong. He believes, as a result of this one failure, that he has lost all his handyman skills and tells himself, "I'm useless. I'll never be able to keep

Table 6.2. Example of Four-Column Records

Event	Thoughts	Feelings	Alternative Thoughts
Forgotten wallet	I'm getting senile.	Frightened	Everyone forgets things occasionally.
An empty mailbox	I'm all alone. Nobody cares.	Sad Isolated	I can't expect a letter when I haven't called or written anyone in a month.
Spouse in nursing home	I've failed as a caretaker.	Inadequate	I haven't failed since he is getting the best care available. Now I can help by visiting.

this place in shape." He feels worthless and incompetent. In another example, a woman feels very depressed one afternoon. She thinks, "My life is nothing but depression these days. I just feel so terrible all the time," and her depression increases. When a man sees a teenager throw garbage on his lawn, he thinks, "Kids nowadays are no good. This neighborhood isn't fit to live in any more." He feels angry and helpless.

In all these examples, the person was assuming that one unpleasant situation applied to all time and to all similar situations and people. This generalization is almost always a distortion of the truth and can best be challenged by looking for exceptions to the overgeneralization. Ask the group members what sort of evidence might the people in the examples find to counteract their overgeneralization (place this evidence in a fourth column on the board).

Personal Application. Overgeneralization can often be detected in the use of words such as *never, always, everyone, no one, all, nobody*. Ask group members to think of a recent time when something bad happened and they thought it would keep on happening or that all people would behave the same way. If they have difficulty in doing this, suggest typical examples such as: "I'm always depressed nowadays," or "No one cares if I live or die." Write these statements and the accompanying dysphoric emotion on the board. Ask members to think of an exception to each overgeneralization and to rephrase their statement in the formula: "It is not true that (*overgeneralization*), because (*exception*)." For example, "It is not true that I can't do anything right, because yesterday I fixed the lamp." Write the corrected statements on the board.

Homework. As usual with cognitive errors, the homework is done in two stages, recognition and challenge. The stages can be combined or assigned on successive weeks, according to the requirements of the members.

For the recognition stage, provide members with an ABC recording sheet and ask them to monitor single distressing incidents, looking in particular for the keywords that indicate overgeneralization. Clients might find it helpful to post a list of keywords in a prominent place as a reminder.

The challenge stage requires members, either at home or during the group session, with or without the help of others, to look for evidence contradicting the overgeneralized conclusion. Members might wish to complete the sentence formula practiced in the group session or simply note the evidence. For this stage of the assignment, members should be asked to complete column D on a form provided. They should also note any change in feelings as a result of the altered thoughts. The records can be shared at the next group session.

Awfulizing

Explanation. In depression, people tend to attach a great deal of importance to unpleasant events in their lives. In fact, they give negative events the power to overshadow and even destroy anything good that might be happening. For example, a woman says, "My daughter was rude to me this morning. It's just terrible that she would treat me that way. It ruins my whole day." Another person complains, "I'm miserable all the time because of my son's marriage." A third person believes, "If I lose any more of my sight, there'll be nothing left for me in life." In all these cases, some unpleasantness really exists, but the people involved are concentrating their time and attention on the negative situation to the exclusion of most other things in life, including anything positive and pleasant. In this way, the negative aspect becomes dominant, with the power to obliterate anything pleasant. Citing these examples, ask group members to identify the words that indicate the exaggerated power each person has given to the negative event.

Personal Application. Awfulizing uses words and phrases such as *terrible, dreadful, awful, tragedy, catastrophe, my day/life etc. is ruined.* Ask members to think of a time, recently, when they felt bad for a while after some occurrence (don't include major events such as death). Write on the board what they said to themselves to exaggerate the importance of the event. Explain that there are several ways to counteract awfulizing:

1. Distract yourself from the negative by noticing something good or pleasant that is also happening: e.g., "My daughter was rude, but I got a nice letter from a friend."
2. See if there is anything good or pleasant in the situation, or any way that it could be made less negative: "At least if I go to a social event alone, I can come home whenever I please, without having to consult with someone else."
3. Decide that it is not your intention to let one negative occurrence ruin your whole day: "I was looking forward to planting my flowers today. I can't do anything about my son's marriage, and I refuse to let thinking about his problems spoil my plans."
4. Accept the negative aspects of the event, but minimize them: "Losing my sight is a very difficult thing for me to handle, but it doesn't mean life is over. I can still talk to people and hear music, and I'm learning how to get around."

Take members' own statements and challenge them, using the above techniques, or another technique the group might invent.

Homework. It is natural to be upset by unpleasant happenings, but they must not be allowed to assume an exaggerated importance if we want to avoid depression. Awfulizing thoughts, especially the small daily ones, need to be challenged. Homework is the same as has been practiced in the Personal Application section of the lecturette. Records should be kept in four columns:

A	B	C	D
Event	Awfulizing + Feeling		Corrective Technique

Mind Reading

Explanation. Mind reading occurs when people assume they know what someone thinks or how someone feels without asking that person. While all people make assumptions about what others think in given situations, these assumptions become a problem when they make the people feel bad. By asking an individual what he or she is thinking or feeling about a situation, misunderstandings that originate in the assumptions can often be cleared up. For example, a man found out that a neighbor was having a party and had invited the whole neighborhood except him. He immediately concluded that the neighbor did not like him and felt rejected. Later, when he found out that the neighbor had tried to reach him, he was relieved and felt embarrassed that he had drawn such a quick conclusion.

To take another case, a woman who had just moved to a new city felt lonely. After several weeks, a neighbor called and invited her to a card party. She declined the invitation because she assumed that the woman only invited her because she was lonely and not because she liked her. Later, she found out that the neighbor really did enjoy her company and she felt disappointed that her mind reading caused her to miss an interesting social occasion.

In these cases, both people mistakenly believed that they could guess what another person was thinking, and their error caused them some distress. Although sometimes, people correctly gauge others' reactions, often they cannot, and they upset themselves unnecessarily.

Suppose, for example, that on a first date Ralph was very quiet. What negative interpretation might Helen, his date, make of his reserved behavior? How might she feel? What other possible (neutral or even positive) explanations might Ralph have for his silence?

Or, take the case of Henry, who had made plans with his wife to go shopping. When the time came for them to leave, she made no mention of the outing and seemed to be involved in an art project of her own. What negative mind reading could Henry do at this point? How would he feel as a result? What other possible explanations are there for the wife's behavior?

In a third example, a man arrives home late for dinner. When he enters the house, his wife frowns at him. What might he believe she is feeling? How might he then feel? Is there any other way to interpret her frown?

Personal Application. Ask members to remember times in their lives when they engaged in negative mind reading, felt unhappy as a result, and discovered later that their interpretations were wrong? Ask them to think of any recent time when they succumbed to negative mind reading, so recent they have not as yet found out whether the suspicions were true? Ask them to think of a more positive mind reading. When people change from negative to positive mind reading, how do their feelings change? Discuss how to check the accuracy of mind reading.

Homework. Mind reading is often hard to detect because it happens so easily. If this type of error in thinking is producing depression, the first step is to gather examples of its occurrence. Ask clients to take a few minutes at the end of each day to look at their interpersonal interactions and at the assumptions they might have made about others' feelings and thoughts. Clients might reevaluate the evidence on which they based an assumption. For example, they could ask themselves, "What made me think he was angry?"

Once it is established that the client is, in fact, mind reading (i.e., drawing a conclusion about another person's feelings or thoughts from nonexistent or flimsy evidence), use the second stage of homework to challenge the mind reading. When possible, check out the mind reading assumption with the person whose mind was "read." When this is not possible, clients can look for evidence that a more positive assumption might be true. In the face of no evidence, they can imagine other possible explanations for the behavior of the person whose mind they are trying to read. These different steps can be presented as separate homework assignments or as one assignment, containing alternative ways to deal with mind reading.

Self-Blame

Explanation. Self-blame is another type of dysfunctional thinking that poses a problem for people with depression. While most people want to see themselves at fault as little as possible, depressed individuals are just the opposite; they try to blame themselves for just about everything. Usually self-blame causes depressed people to feel even more depressed.

Excessive self-blame can be challenged in at least two ways: One is to ask oneself whether this amount of blame would seem reasonable if someone else blamed himself or herself that much. Another way is to wonder if one is being greedy in claiming all the blame. In other words, was anyone else to blame in any way, and how big a share of the blame should one legitimately claim?

For example, a woman whose husband had a severely debilitating disease blamed herself for not having learned about nutritional approaches to the prevention of the disease. She told herself that it was her fault that her husband was so ill; she had been a terrible wife. She felt so guilty that she, too, became ill.

In another example, a man who prided himself on his financial success lost a great deal of money in the stock market. He told himself that he should have foreseen the disaster; it was his fault that his family's financial situation had deteriorated. These thoughts made him feel so depressed that he was unable to work, and the situation got worse. In both these cases, some self-blame might be legitimate, but both people increased their depression by blaming themselves and by dwelling on their faults.

Suppose a man were to find out that his wife was having an affair. How might he unreasonably blame himself? What would his feelings be if he accepted all the blame? Or suppose a woman finds out that she has been tricked out of her savings by a con man. She would naturally feel very upset by this. How might she make herself feel even worse by blaming herself?

Personal Application. Ask members to think of times when they blamed themselves and felt very bad as a result. One way to think of occasions is to complete the sentence, "It's my fault that . . . " Ask them, "How large a share of the blame do you think is yours? Can you think of anyone else or any other factors that might share the responsibility? How much blame would you apportion to someone else in a similar situation?"

During this discussion, group members can be asked to estimate how much blame should be allotted in each case. It is often enlightening to members to discover that almost everyone has different opinions on the subject.

Homework. Because it is so natural to look for a culprit when trouble arises, it is sometimes hard to realize when people blame themselves too much, especially if others are happy to agree and let them have all the blame. If excessive self-blame is a hidden problem, one way to gain a better perspective on it is by exaggerating it. For the first level of homework, ask clients to list all the negative events of each day and find a way to blame themselves for each one. If there seem to be no problems, that can be a cause for self-blame, too, because clients can accuse themselves of not trying hard enough to do their homework.

A second level of homework is to ask clients to examine present and past incidents of self-blame, listing all other possible factors and people that could reasonably share the blame. The clients need not be convinced of the contribution of these factors, but should bring in the list, so that the group can help the person sort out how much self-blame is responsible.

Demands on Others

Explanation. It is natural for all of us to anticipate things and to feel disappointed when our expectations are not met. This disappointment can turn to depression when we require, or demand, that things happen or people behave in a certain way. To prefer or wish that things go as we would like them to is reasonable, but people set themselves up for depression when they *expect* others to think or feel or act as they would prefer. When people feel let down by others, they often make the situation worse by the conclusions they draw. They might decide, for example, that the other person is in some way bad and, as a result, alienate themselves from that person. It is even more depressing if they conclude that the other person disappointed them because of their own failing. For example, a man raised his children to be Roman Catholics. When they left the Catholic Church, he was so angry and disappointed that he refused to allow them in his house. This man made three errors in thinking that led to his depression: First, he expected his children to espouse his values rather than develop beliefs of their own. Second, he concluded that his children were sinful. And third, he concluded that their lack of faith reflected on him and meant that he had done a poor job as a father. A woman who prized books lent one to a friend who had little respect for books. The friend returned it with coffee stains on the cover. The lender made the same three types of mistakes in her thinking: "She should know better than to treat my property like that" (expecting her friend to have the same values as she had). "She's irresponsible and untrustworthy" (drawing negative conclusions about the person's character). "She obviously doesn't think I'm worth having as a friend" (drawing negative conclusions about herself). These thoughts and the consequent feelings led to a permanent rift in the friendship. Demanding that others live by one's standards will almost always lead to depression, because there are many different standards of behavior in the world and few people are likely to have exactly the same standards.

Several methods can counteract the "shoulds" that occur when people demand that others behave as they think they ought. One way is to realize that there are many different standards in the world and no way to prove which is right. This realization can be achieved by asking others to discuss their rules and beliefs on various topics. Even the group often contains a considerable diversity of opinion, at least enough to counter the common belief that "everyone knows . . . [or] everyone believes . . . " Another way is to talk with others to examine their expectations to see if they are reasonable. For example, a widowed mother expected her busy married son to visit her daily. In what ways might this be too much to expect? Is there possibly a compromise that mother and son could agree on? Sometimes, the "rule" is quite reasonable but the other person chooses not to follow it. As there is no way to force others to follow one's own wishes, it can be helpful in these situations to examine the conclusions drawn. For example, a son expected his parents to pay for his college education, whereas *they* believed that he would value his education more if he had to work for it. The son risked depression and alienation if he concluded, "This proves that they don't think I'm worth their love. I must be unimportant to them. They are terrible people and I want nothing more to do with them." People can be helped to identify their conclusions and ask themselves: "Is there another way to explain the behavior?" "Does just one act mean that the whole person is worthless?" "Even if the person *is* terrible, why should that say anything bad about me?"

Personal Application. To recognize when one demands that others live by one's beliefs and rules, look for the words *should, ought, must,* or statements that tell others how to behave: for example, "If you loved me, you would . . . " or "If you were a good son to me you wouldn't . . . " Explain to the members, "Another way to tell if you are demanding is by your reactions. When the person did not do as you expected, were you merely disappointed or did you feel angry, betrayed, hurt, helpless? If these were your reactions, you probably had an unreasonable expectation that the other person would comply with your wishes."

Ask them to think of a time when they were disappointed by someone else's behavior. "What belief or rule were you demanding that person follow? What assumption did you make about shared values or opinions? When the person did not do things as you expected, how strong were your reactions? What conclusions did you draw about the other person's character or about yourself?" Discussion of the rules underlying demands can be valuable if group members are able to help a person to identify rules that are unreasonable or can suggest compromises.

Homework. During the coming week, ask members to monitor their feelings regarding how others treat them or behave in general, and notice if they are saying or implying a "should." Have them bring a record of those feelings to the next session. Second level homework concerns deciding whether to keep or discard a particular standard for the behavior of others. To make this decision, it can be helpful to consult others whom one respects. One possibility is to role play, in the group session, an interaction to be carried out for homework, in which someone negotiates a compromise with someone else or discusses a problematic behavior. It is also possible to break the intensity of an emotional reaction by reminding oneself, "I can't expect everyone else to think the way I do. People have a right to live their own way" (providing, of course, that the client endorsed this belief and arrived at it without undue persuasion by the therapist or other group members).

Unrealistic Expectations of Self

Explanation. As people mature, they develop standards for their own behavior and attendant expectations of how they will and should behave in various situations. Those who fail to live up to these expectations often feel ashamed or guilty, and the uncomfortable feelings push them to make amends for any harm done or to try harder in the future. Thus, self-expectations are a good way to keep behavior in line. However, feeling upset about one's performance can become a problem. Depressed people tend to make two mistakes in the area of self-expectations: First, they often set up unrealistically high standards for themselves, and second, they are unforgiving toward themselves when they do not meet these standards.

For example, a man lost his job because of illness and could not provide for his family as well as before. His upset over his unemployment turned to depression because he kept telling himself, "I should be able to take care of my family. I shouldn't let my health stop me. If I were a strong person, I'd get over these problems." Similarly, a woman, unable to care at home for her husband who had a stroke, put him in a nursing home. She became depressed by telling herself what a terrible wife she was because she should be able to look after him. In both examples, the people made themselves depressed because they were demanding the impossible from themselves.

Most unrealistic self-expectations are based on a set of rules about how one "should" behave as a good husband, wife, child, parent, employer, etc. Often these rules become an automatic part of thinking, and are rarely examined as to whether they make sense in a particular situation. In the examples just mentioned, the unemployed man had a rule that a man must always provide for his family or else he is a failure. The woman had a rule that a woman always takes care of her family's physical ailments, and she is a failure if she does not. Neither of these people allowed for exceptions to their rules, caused by uncontrollable circumstances.

Personal Application. Take the example of a woman who became depressed because her real estate company was doing badly during a severe slump in the housing market. What unrealistic self-expectations (that is, what "shoulds" or "rules") might she be telling herself about her performance as a business woman? In another case, a salesman could find no other job that paid as well as selling, although he had to spend most of his time away from home. His teenage son was arrested for drug dealing. What unrealistic rules might the father have about his role—rules that could lead to depression?

There are several ways to challenge rules that lead to depression. First, ask others if they have the same rule and if they allow any exceptions. Often, other people have very different rules, yet still manage to be decent, responsible human beings. This realization can help members feel free to choose a less harsh rule or to forgive themselves. Second, ask whether breaking one rule really means that one is a complete failure in that area. For example, is putting a sick husband in a nursing home proof that someone is a bad wife, or are there some other ways to be a good spouse? Third, ask if the same rule would apply to other people. Often, people set higher standards for themselves than others, almost as if they were, somehow, better than others to start with and can, therefore, be expected to reach higher. Members could ask themselves what reason they have to think they are so different from others.

In order for members to look at any of their own rules—rules that might be contributing to their depression—have them think of a time when they were disappointed or upset with their own behavior and felt they should have acted differently. What "should" or "rule" did they have? Using one of the approaches just discussed, have them examine their rule and see if it was unrealistic or if they were being too hard on themselves.

Homework. Like many other depressing thoughts, "should" and "oughts" are often automatic. The first step to eliminating these thoughts is to become aware of them. Ask clients to record each occasion on which they feel disappointed, upset, angry, or frustrated with themselves and to identify the underlying demands they are making on themselves. Discuss these records with the group during the next session. If clients are unable to identify their underlying demands, they could be asked to list the various roles they play in life, together with a set of rules for each role by completing sentences such as "A good father . . . " "A Christian . . . " "A responsible citizen . . . "

The second level of homework is for clients to challenge their "shoulds".

Since "shoulds" are often the product of a lifetime set of values, many older adults will not wish to abandon even those that might appear unrealistic. In these cases, therapists can reach a compromise by focusing on the idea of accepting the occasional failure, continuing to do one's best and perhaps trying to compensate for failure in other ways. Several of our older group members, though unwilling to relax their standards, were able to endorse the statement, "I'm doing the best I can, even if I make mistakes."

Exaggerating Self-Importance

Explanation. A type of distorted thinking that increases depression is exaggerating one's self-importance. This usually occurs in social situations where the person thinks that others are watching or thinking about him or her. This type of error in thinking can be recognized in phrases such as "Everyone noticed . . . " "Everyone knows I did that wrong . . . " "They are all thinking . . . " This error is based in the belief that one is the center of other people's attention and that they are all noticing and criticizing one's mistakes. Two ways to challenge the belief are to check out whether, in fact, everyone noticed and, even if they did, what importance should be given to their noticing.

For example, a man entered a crowded dining room, caught his heel on the step and fell. His immediate thought was, "Everyone saw me fall. They must think I'm drunk." Feeling embarrassed and conspicuous, he at once left the room, not looking at anyone. In another example, a woman who was usually meticulous about her writing mailed out a Christmas letter to her friends and only later noticed several misspellings. She thought, "Everyone will think I'm losing my mind", and was so mortified and ashamed that she lost all pleasure at the prospect of talking with her friends over Christmas time.

Personal Application. In what ways might the following people upset themselves by exaggerating their self-importance? A man, usually a careful dresser, spills gravy on his tie before a business meeting; he has no time to change his tie. A woman loses her temper with her 2-year old in church and swats him because he won't stay seated.

Ask members to think of a recent social situation when they felt embarrassed or the object of everyone's attention for a mistake they made. What were their thoughts? Did they have any evidence that everyone noticed the mistake or did they just assume that? Even if everyone did notice, what negative conclusion could they draw about what happened? Did they have any evidence that these conclusions were indeed drawn? In a social situation, how much time do *they* spend looking at others and criticizing their behavior?

It can be particularly valuable to use the group to challenge this type of cognitive error. Members are often willing to discuss an aspect of themselves or their behavior that they assume the other group members have noticed. One member, for example, had refused for some time to dine out because of an uncontrollable tremor in his hand. In group he apologized, under his breath, for the way that papers shook in his hand. When he checked with others, he was surprised to hear that most of them had neither heard his mutterings nor noticed the tremor. The discussion had a double benefit for him. He began to eat out without embarrassment, and he also stopped (in group at least) an annoying habit of pointing out mistakes that others made.

Homework. Often it is difficult to realize how concerned people are about what others think, so it takes careful monitoring of thoughts and feelings to find situations where this type of thinking interferes with one's life.

This week, after the group members have spent some time with other people, have them go back over the occasion and ask if at any time they were worried about negative thoughts others had about them, as a result of any *faux pas* they made. Have them record the thoughts and feelings they had; these will be discussed later.

A second level of homework involves two types of challenge. One is to learn to identify when members feel that all eyes are upon them, to look for evidence that they are, indeed, the center of attention. They could also use a personalized self-statement to counter their discomfort; for example, "Most people are too busy with their own affairs to pay that much attention to me," "So what if they notice? Everyone makes mistakes occasionally. It's nothing to be ashamed of," or "Only critical people concern themselves about mistakes others make. I don't value such unkindness, so their opinion is unimportant to me."

Another type of challenge for this cognitive error involves exploration of situations where a person's behavior is constrained because of anticipated social disapproval. In these situations, the person is always on edge, afraid of doing the wrong thing, and as a result, does not relax or feel accepted in company. To identify these situations, members should look for social events that they avoid or leave early, and investigate any cognitions about self-importance.

CONTACT WORK

Individual contact work with members of the group is designed to intensify the therapeutic experience and to engage clients maximally in the problem-solving process. These individualized experiences are designed to provide greater impact and mobilize the clients' energies toward problem resolution. Because it relies on self-discovery and involves more of the client's emotional resources, contact work is a major focus of the change phase. Contact work is conducted on a one-to-one basis as in phase two, but the main difference is that the focus is on actively making changes rather than on identification of cognitive errors.

Purpose and Benefits

The primary purpose of contact work is to focus an individual client's energies upon the pattern of cognitive response that has been destructive to his or her own existence. Individual contact work begins with the identification of disturbing and destructive cognitions and proceeds to developing alternative thoughts. This procedure benefits the group members as well as the targeted individual, with whom the therapist is working. Targeted clients receive benefit because of the individualized attention, which facilitates the collaborative spirit as well as concentrates on the unique permutations and characteristics of their own peculiar dilemma. For the group members, the benefit is derived through observation, imitation, and cognitive instruction.

Procedure

1. Individuals wishing particular attention can place their names and problems on the agenda for the group session. From this agenda, an individual is selected and invited to do contact work. *Example*: During homework rounds Mabel reported that she had been unable to complete her self-assigned homework task of preparing her taxes for the accountant. She asked that this problem be placed on the agenda for contact work later in the session.

2. Contact work is based primarily on the development of the A-B-C model. It is usually helpful to begin with having the client either identify A (the situation in provoking their feelings) or C (the problematic feelings or behavior). The client is asked to describe these feelings and the attendant situations. This information is recorded on the board or on a note pad that the client can see. At times, therapists need to clarify distinctions between feelings and thoughts. For example, clients often identify their thoughts as "feelings" (e.g., "I feel like my children do not care about me"). The therapist reports this as a "thought" rather than as a feeling. *Example*: When the therapist sat down with Mabel to delineate the problem, two different situations emerged as problems, each with its attendant thoughts and feelings. Mabel felt overwhelmed, inadequate, and panicky when she tried to do her taxes, and embarrassed and hopeless when she reported on her "failure" to the group.

3. The client is asked to make a rating of the intensity of his or her feelings. *Example*: On a 10-point scale (10 being the greatest intensity), Mabel rated the feelings arising at home from trying to do taxes as much higher than the feelings she had in group. On the basis of her strong emotions and the imminence of April 15, Mabel decided that it would be more valuable for her to concentrate on the difficulty with taxes rather than on her discussion of the problem in group.

4. The client is asked to explore the beliefs about the situation that seem to evoke the feelings and accompanying behavior. As these beliefs are described, the therapist records them. *Example*: As well as helping the client to identify automatic thoughts, the therapist will try to categorize the thought according to the type of error. One way to do this is to offer for the client's consideration a summary statement of the automatic thoughts, expressed in the form of a cognitive error. For example, Sam has thoughts indicating that he is unsure of his abilities. The therapist asks about the belief underlying the insecurity: "Does this situation mean to you that you are a failure? Could it be that you believe this situation proves that it is not worth living if you can't accomplish a simple task? Is this just another example to you of how life always puts you down?" By this stage of therapy, leaders usually have sufficient knowledge of clients to be able to zero in on the content and style of underlying beliefs likely to fit for each person.

In the example of Mabel, three main thoughts and underlying beliefs were identified.

Cognition	*Underlying Belief*	*Type of Error*
This is too confusing.	I must be senile.	Overgeneralizing.
I can't handle it.	I should be able to cope with this.	Unreasonable self-expectations.
It'll be too late!	It's a disaster if it's not done by April 15.	Catastrophizing.

5. The therapist, working collaboratively with the client, makes the determination of which of the various beliefs and assumptions described most strongly contributes to the disruptive feelings and behavior. *Example*: Since Mabel's panic and catastrophizing thoughts caused her the greatest distress, she and the therapist decided to focus contact work on that issue.

6. Typically, the client is now asked to rate the degree of his or her belief in the problematic attitude or assumption. *Example*: When asked to rate her belief that not completing taxes by April 15 would be a disaster, Mabel emphatically claimed 99% belief.

7. The next step is to implement an intervention: to question the veracity of the belief, to construct some hypotheses about the significance and nature of that belief, or to explore the origins of the belief. This intervention is undertaken in a questioning stance, allowing and encouraging the client to derive his or her own conclusions about the nature of the belief and its veracity. The following questions are helpful in directing this exploration: (a) Is the assumption true or has it ever not been true? (b) How else can one view or interpret the situation or how would others view it? (c) Is the anticipated consequence likely to be as bad as it seems? (d) Is there some other explanation of the situation? (e) How likely is the anticipated consequence to occur? (Other questions can be found in Table 6.1.) Each of these questions is directed at a different aspect or type of cognitive distortion. In the course of this exploration, clients are typically also asked to evaluate their evidence for maintaining their belief. In this process, clients are asked to describe the basis on which their belief rests and to explore any evidence that might exist to counteract or contradict their belief systems. *Example*: When the therapist asked Mabel for her evidence that not completing taxes would be a disaster, she said that her husband always took the task very seriously and used to tell her that "all you have to do in life is die and pay taxes." She had no other evidence and did not know the reasons for her husband's belief. When asked what she thought might be the disastrous consequences, she said she believed she could be sent to prison. At this point, the therapist encouraged Mabel to question the other members about their knowledge of the consequences of not doing taxes on time. Someone told Mabel about filing an extension.

8. At this point, clients are asked to provide feedback about how their belief systems have changed and to rerate the belief on the same type of scale used at the initiation of the procedure. *Example*: By the time she had talked to the group, Mabel rerated her belief as 4, since she still had lingering doubts about the propriety of a decent citizen asking for an extension, but she believed her panic to be sufficiently reduced that she might be able to take action on her taxes.

9. The next step is designed to assist clients to translate their new knowledge and the explorations recently undertaken by applying them to a homework assignment. Homework assignments can be designed either to (a) check out existing beliefs that the client is still evaluating, or (b) practice a new belief derived from the contact work when the same situation arises. *Example*: Mabel had two homework assignments. The first was to get an extension on her taxes, and another group member offered to help her do this. The second was designed to deal with her recurring panic. When she felt panicky about not being punctual with her taxes, Mabel agreed to tell herself, "It can't be such a bad thing to be late with taxes if they have a law made especially for that situation."

Homework

The overall objective of homework assigned after contact work is for clients to evaluate their perceptions and to develop more realistic ones. It is assumed that when clients obtain evidence that contradicts their beliefs, their perceptions will change. Clients might be asked to act differently and observe their reactions in order to check certain kinds of evidence (e.g., "see what happens if you act as if your son cares about you rather than as if he does not"). The client might also be asked to look for evidence contrary to a belief (e.g., "I wonder if you would be willing to observe how many people in your family make nice or encouraging comments to you this week—simply count the number of times that people express affection or support"). Individuals who have come to recognize that alternative thoughts might be more realistic than beliefs previously held could be asked to practice the new thoughts periodically throughout the week at designated times, keyed either by their own discomfort or by the social situation.

Discussion

Frequently clients approach individual contact work with some trepidation at being "on center stage." The tactic we have come to adopt is simply to encourage people to face their fears, take a risk, and begin some initial exploration. It is advantageous for the therapist to move from group member to group member, rather than establishing a "hot seat," as some therapeutic procedures encourage. Hence, clients remain seated in their most comfortable positions, while therapists move from individual to individual.

Following each segment of contact work, the identified client is asked how she or he feels about the work. Group members are then asked to provide their comments, thoughts, and assistance; these comments often help the client identify more rational alternative beliefs and provide support for changes made. Such processing can also be used to help those group members who observed the procedure to apply it to themselves. That is, group members can be provided with a list of questions that were relevant to defining the problematic cognition in the targeted client and asked to apply these same questions to problems of their own.

It is in part through the group feedback following individual contact work that the group maintains cohesiveness, collaboration, and mutual support. By being aware that all group members will be asked to engage in the process, initial fears about it may be easily overcome.

BEHAVIORAL TECHNIQUES

In the change phase, behavioral techniques are frequently used as an adjunct to the homework assignments emanating from individual contact work. The behavioral techniques most often used in this manner are stimulus control and behavioral rehearsal.

Stimulus Control

Stimulus control procedures involve the arrangement or rearrangement of specific environmental conditions, and they can be adapted especially for use in the treatment of depressed older adults.

Purpose and Benefits. The emotional manifestations of depression— feelings of sadness, hopelessness, loneliness, guilt, etc.—and cognitive manifestations—such as worry, self-blame, and pessimism—are often triggered or exacerbated by environmental stimuli. Many older adults live and move in rather restricted and unvarying circumstances, as a result they come into frequent contact with the same stimuli. They also tend to surround themselves with reminders of the past and of their often distant or alienated family and friends. Thus, they are particularly vulnerable to the impact of environmental stimuli, more so, for example, than a younger person who has either more distractions, such as children to care for, or more variety, such as employment. For older adults, the photographs of a deceased spouse, the souvenirs of happy occasions in the past, the dozens of medication bottles, and the craftwork left unfinished are ever-present and powerful triggers of depressive feelings and thoughts.

The purposes of stimulus control procedures are to weaken or eliminate undesirable responses by setting up environmental conditions that make it impossible or unlikely for the undesired emotion or cognition to occur and to strengthen desirable responses by arranging the environment so as to increase the likelihood of these responses.

Stimulus control techniques have an intuitive appeal for most people, as they represent a commonsense method of self-management that is in everyday use. Few of us have not used an alarm clock, or placed a letter that needs to be mailed by the door. The deliberate use of these techniques to control depressive symptoms is merely a more elaborate way of doing what most nondepressed people do almost automatically, in an attempt to behave more adaptively. Some advantages of stimulus control are that it is an easy technique for older adults to understand and use, it can be effective in controlling specific depressive thoughts and feelings, and it promotes in people a sense of being in control of their lives.

Procedure. The following steps are characteristically followed in implementing stimulus control strategies.

1. One should provide a rationale for stimulus control which includes the following points: (a) What you see and hear around you, in your environment, can set off certain thoughts resulting in dysfunctional feelings; (b) When these thoughts and feelings are ones that cause you distress, you can sometimes change the feelings by changing your environment; (c) Chances are that changing your environment in order to control your own behavior is something you have been doing for years. For example, you might have set a letter to be mailed on the hall table; (d) What we will be learning today is simply a more systematic method of control from what you already know.

2. Clients are asked to identify a target feeling they would like to eliminate or reduce in intensity that is prompted by an environmental setting.

3. Clients are then assisted in describing the target in one specific situation, such as "I feel sad whenever I see my husband's overcoat hanging in the hall closet," or "I feel lonely when I walk into church by myself."

4. Next, clients are asked to identify which stimuli enhance the target feeling and which inhibit it. This process might necessitate that the client keep a record of the occurrences of the target feelings, including a description of the physical environment in which the target responses occur.

5. Therapists should then work out a plan with each client to engineer the environment in order to eliminate or suppress the cues that trigger the undesirable responses.

Discussion. Target responses need not, of course, be limited to emotions; thoughts and behavior can be used as well. The first target response clients try to change should be a relatively simple, reactive one in order to facilitate learning the principles of stimulus control. Later on, when clients understand and have some facility in using the techniques, more complex target responses can be used.

In the final procedural step, when an environmental engineering plan is being devised, other group members can be used as resources since they are often more familiar than the therapist with the stimuli likely to both trigger and calm strong emotions.

Each person's environment is composed of other people, who can both function as cues to unwanted behaviors and be used as part of an engineered environment. Older adults have little difficulty in recognizing the wisdom of avoiding or at least limiting their contact with people who, for example, feed their sadness by continually reminiscing about the happier days in the past. They are also adept at solving practical problems. For example, one may suggest that if going to church alone is the target response, this cue to feeling isolated and abandoned can be eliminated by arranging to ride to church with a friend or by attaching oneself to acquaintances in the parking lot and walking up the path with them.

Behavior Rehearsal

In behavior rehearsal the client practices, within group therapy, a novel and appropriate response to a problem situation. A suitable response is selected collaboratively by therapist and client; this response is modeled and then practiced until it can be performed skillfully. For example, a woman who is intimidated by her physician might rehearse asking to have her medication changed. Corrective feedback on the performance is provided, and the therapist encourages the client to carry out these planned actions in the natural setting, where they are most likely to result in positive reinforcement.

Purpose and Benefits. Although role playing is used for a variety of purposes, including assessment, attitude change, and catharsis, the goal of behavior rehearsal is to help clients acquire interpersonal skills. Although, in the course of many years of interaction with others, most older adults have acquired the skills to deal with familiar situations, aging often brings new interpersonal situations that require unfamiliar response patterns.

Behavior rehearsal can be of help to older adults in a variety of situations. Many older adults find it difficult to communicate with their physicians. They complain that their doctors talk to their relatives, not to them, that they don't answer questions, don't explain possible reactions to medications, and don't give them their full attention (Commerford, 1984). Behavior rehearsal can be an excellent way of learning how to cope with difficult situations such as this, by practicing more effective methods of asking questions and demanding information. Interpersonal interactions with well-meaning relatives who try to take charge of or direct the client are also a frequent problem for older adults. A man might use behavior rehearsal to practice suitable methods of telling his daughter that he wants to live in his own apartment, whether or not the daughter thinks it is safe. Behavior rehearsal affords an environment in which to practice and explore new ways of responding without undue concern for the negative consequences that might accompany these halting and unskilled efforts in the real world. Behavior rehearsal is an especially valuable technique in a group setting, because the other members of the group can provide a variety of suggestions on how to handle a given situation as well as social reinforcement for improved performance.

Many depressed persons hold unrealistically negative expectations about the reactions of others. These expectations are seldom contradicted because their presence causes clients to avoid the situations that would test them. By rehearsing a situation in the group and having the support of the group members, a client is more likely to summon up the courage to attempt an interpersonal interaction that has been avoided. Once the client attempts the new situation, the accuracy of his or her beliefs can be assessed. If other people do not react as expected, this experience can be explored as evidence that the client's cognitions are faulty, inaccurate, and need revision in the face of new evidence.

Procedure. Before beginning the rehearsal, the client must recognize the need for learning a new response. Time and care must be taken with this first step, as the client might not view the difficulty as a deficiency in interpersonal skills but as a problem belonging to another person, as a sign of the times, or as a manifestation of a global personality trait or demographic variable (e.g., "Nobody likes old people," "I'm no fun to be with," "Nobody bothers with anyone these days, they're all too busy rushing around"). In presenting behavior rehearsal, therefore, the following steps are followed:

1. The group is presented with a rationale for using behavior rehearsal, emphasizing the safety of the group situation and the value of practice.

2. A target situation likely to occur during the coming week is selected. A situation should be chosen in which the interaction will be initiated by the client, so that the client retains control of whether to practice in vivo what is learned in therapy.

3. The therapist works with the client to clarify the situation, finding out the details of the upcoming situation (where and when it will be, who else will be there, etc.), what the client wants to happen, what the client is afraid will happen, and how the client has handled similar situations in the past.

4. At some point it will be necessary to decide whether the problem results from a skill deficit or cognitive distortions about probable consequences. Often, elderly depressed clients have specific thoughts that prevent them from taking appropriate action they have previously exhibited. These self-defeating cognitions include such examples as, "There's no point in speaking up, he won't listen to me anyway," "They're awfully busy, they won't have time for me if I call," and "They don't want old people at those meetings." If a distortion of the client's cognitions, and not a deficit in skills, is inhibiting action then the therapist might best work on modifying those cognitions rather than on rehearsing the problem situation. For example, an elderly woman in one of our groups was reluctant to ask her apartment manager to repair her frontdoor lock, because

doing so would "cause him too much inconvenience." With the enthusiastic help of the group members, she recognized that a broken front-door lock was a dangerous situation that should not continue, that the apartment manager was paid to see that the door locks were in working order, and that he might very well be eager to repair the lock but could not do so if he did not know it was broken. Once she had changed her belief about the appropriateness of the action, she was easily able to make the request. Rehearsal was not needed.

5. If a skill deficit does exist and behavior rehearsal is agreed upon, the next step is to construct roles for other group members to play. In helping clients define appropriate roles, the therapist should find out from the targeted client how others in the situation are likely to behave, so that those playing the other roles can act realistically.

6. It is also helpful to elicit information from the client regarding the nature of the physical environment (table, chairs, other people involved, etc.) and to set the scene, making certain that the actors are positioned so that all group members can see and hear them.

7. Serving as director, the therapist then instructs the client and other actors to rehearse the problem situation. The client is asked to practice the new response several times according to the plan.

8. After the situation has been rehearsed, the therapist arranges for the client to receive feedback by first asking the client to evaluate his or her own performance and inquiring how he or she felt about it. If a considerable amount of anxiety was experienced, the rehearsal should be repeated.

9. The roles and situation are then selectively modified both to accommodate variations that might occur and to eliminate improbable elements. In most cases, after three or four rehearsals, the anxiety has diminished sufficiently to allow the client to try the behavior in real life. The leaders might then evaluate the client's performance before the group members make comments, in order to model how to give specific, positive feedback in which the client is told precisely what he or she did well and how to phrase negative feedback as specific suggestions for improvement. It is the intent of such modeling to help group members give feedback that will be received more positively than it would otherwise have been, in order to be as helpful as possible to the client.

10. When the rehearsal has been successful, the client's homework assignment should be to try out the behavior in real life during the coming week.

Discussion. A number of difficulties are likely to arise when conducting behavior rehearsal with the elderly. One of the most important is keeping the session on task. Most people, older adults in particular, are apt to want to spend their time talking about the difficulties of the problem situation rather than devising and practicing new ways of responding to it. The client often has not had an opportunity to talk about the troubling situation and, consequently, feels a great need to tell the group about it. Furthermore, the act of rehearsing behavior is unfamiliar to most clients, and they feel shy and awkward when practicing in front of a group; they are much more comfortable sitting and talking about the situation. It is sometimes helpful, as a first step, to have a reluctant client describe the situation and to have the leaders or other group members play the client's part. The client is more likely to be willing to rehearse the situation after this modeling exercise.

If rehearsing is still too threatening, the leaders might elect to break the rehearsal plan into small steps and ask the client to practice only a small portion of the situation at a time, using guided imagery before trying to engage in overt interactions. For example, if a six-step plan has been created to help a client tell her son that she wants to live on her own, the client might begin by practicing only the step of letting her son know she wants to talk with him ("John, there's something important I want to talk with you about"). Even a very frightened client is usually able to practice verbal dialogues, one sentence at a time. After several one-sentence rehearsals, the client is often willing to combine these exchanges into a full-blown rehearsal; but even if not, the one-sentence rehearsals themselves are likely to be of some help.

Another difficulty for the therapist is developing a procedure to efficiently gather the relevant and important information before beginning the rehearsal. The major problem with most therapists' attempts at directing behavior rehearsal is that they fail to find out the precise nature of the problem before they intervene. It is not an easy task to discover what happened before, how often, when, with whom, what the client did, what the other people involved did, and how the client wants similar situations to turn out in the future. And, it must be done rapidly enough that the other members of the group do not get bored. It is helpful to write the questions on a blackboard, so the group members can see what questions need to be answered, and to solicit the coleader's help in keeping the group members on track.

The extent to which the group members should be used in a single client's behavior rehearsal is an important decision, to be based on the clinician's judgment of several factors that vary from group to group. On the one hand, it is interesting and in many ways beneficial to use the group members to help design the rehearsal plan, to play other relevant characters in the problem situation, and when the rehearsal is finished, to give the client evaluative feedback on his or her performance. Discovering and changing the client's problem situation, in essence, becomes a group project. The client gets a great deal of support, and the other group members feel more a part of the therapy. On the other hand, not all elderly depressed clients are ready to participate in such a group project, and there is great potential for misfortune. For example, when asked for appropriate responses in the problem situation, members might remain silent, take the opportunity to tell a largely irrelevant story, or state bluntly that no response whatsoever will work. Group participants might not volunteer to play the roles of the other people in the situation or might not do an adequate job if they do volunteer, and their feedback, despite excellent modeling by the therapists, might be uselessly vague or entirely negative. The clinician must read the group's tone and estimate the probability of negative and positive effects, perhaps experimenting with different amounts and ways of involving group members.

An important procedural variation to use in conducting a behavioral rehearsal is to focus on the client's nonverbal behavior. Tone of voice, pace of speech, latency of response, gestures, eye contact, posture, etc., can play a significant part in effective interpersonal skills. When nonverbal factors are critical, the entire rehearsal from creation of the plan to the feedback can be structured to focus on nonverbal skills. In doing so, videotape equipment can be very useful to help clients to see themselves as others see them.

FINAL NOTE

The change phase of cognitive therapy is the meat of the entire treatment process. During this phase, clients are taught to actively engage their own problems, to develop a questioning attitude to assumptions they've held throughout life, and to design new means of perceiving and evaluating the situations that provide and produce stress. It should not be underemphasized, however, that the group provides important support and collaboration in this endeavor. The process should be one of self-exploration, with the therapist providing as little direct recommendation as possible. The skilled therapist, however, can capitalize both on the information and suggestions provided by other group members and on the client's own self-exploratory process to direct the client to a helpful, beneficial conclusion.

Chapter 7
Phase Four: Consolidation/Termination

Cognitive therapy groups are time limited; the group will end at a pre-determined date. This limitation allows leaders to prepare for termination in several different ways and at different stages of the group. It is important that leaders allow several sessions to work through the termination process and obtain closure, since too abrupt a transition from the group experience, with its support and education, to an independent life can result in a rapid loss of therapeutic gains.

Participants will, of course, be informed during the selection interview of the group's termination date and, as this date approaches, additional references should be made to it with comments such as, "We only have five weeks left in group" or "The group will be ending just two weeks before your daughter's wedding." In this way, the end of the group becomes an integral part of each member's life, and ambiguity and surprise are reduced. In a 20-week group, an increasing amount of time could be spent on termination issues from about the 15th session.

A practical method of helping participants adjust to the fact that they need to go on without the group is called *thinning* or *fading* in the behavioral literature. This means simply that instead of having the group continue to meet weekly until the final session, the last few sessions are scheduled every other week or even every third week. This process incorporates trial periods of independence with regular group therapy. Leaders might also schedule follow-up group sessions, 3, 6, or even 12 months after termination of the group, in order to help group members with difficulties they had during the intervening time and to reinforce the maintenance of skills and additional learning. Group members can meet on their own at "reunions" to facilitate a sense of support and involvement. And, of course, leaders should make it clear to the participants that if, at the end of group, they still need additional therapy, the leaders will make every effort to refer them to suitable group or individual therapy. Further, group members should be reassured that if at any time in

106

the future serious problems arise, they are welcome to telephone the leaders for consultation about treatment.

The purposes of the consolidation/termination phase are (a) to help group members consolidate the gains they made in the group, (b) to teach them how to maintain those gains, and (c) to assist them in separating from the group. In general, new concepts are not introduced during this final phase, the assumption being that members have already learned all the material the therapists deem appropriate and are now focused on the practice and refinement of skills and concepts acquired thus far. This shift in emphasis frequently results in a departure from the agenda pattern followed in earlier sessions. It is likely that, during the final phase, there will be few if any lecturettes, since these are largely a device to introduce new material. Consequently, homework will not be planned in advance as part of a lecturette, but will be derived ad hoc from group discussions or from individual contact work.

During this final stage, the members' lives outside and beyond the group command most of the attention. The importance of homework increases and much of a session might be devoted to debriefing the previous week's work and preparing for the next homework. Typically, during the last sessions, therapists encourage increasing interaction among members, whose receding depression allows for such involvement and who have generally learned how to provide each other with helpful feedback, suggestions, and reinforcement. Thus, the emphasis of the sessions anticipates and mirrors a condition of self-management and interaction with others, without constant therapist intervention. In essence, members spend this last phase working on individual treatment plans that will enable them to maximize their therapeutic experience.

CONSOLIDATION OF
THERAPY GAINS

Clients need to learn two processes in order to maintain the gains made in the cognitive therapy group. The first process is specifying and reinforcing the therapeutic gains that they made. The second process is learning to anticipate and address new, potentially depressive situations. Partial accomplishment of both steps can be achieved when therapists help clients develop a more generalized view of their depressive themes. Although depressed people are likely to commit several different cognitive errors, a pattern of underlying assumptions or *schema* (Beck et al., 1979) individualistically characterizes each person. For example, some people consistently hold self-expectations that are too high across various situations, others have a pervasive tendency to blame others. During this final phase of therapy, consolidation of gains can be helped through the discovery of these themes, or underlying cognitive schema, that predispose an individual to make the same mistakes over and over.

If the previous three phases of therapy were successful, clients learned to place their dysfunctional thoughts into the various cognitive error categories, determined which errors they make most frequently, and learned to evaluate and change specific cognitive patterns. With this information, therapists now can help clients explore more basic and broad-ranging assumptions about themselves, others, and the world. Other group members can be of assistance in this task; having listened to each other in group for many weeks, they are often able to start with such generalized observations as, "I've noticed that you get really upset when you make a mistake. You seem to be hard on yourself, and think you should always do everything perfectly." It can be explained that, sometimes, these recurrent patterns represent generalized life attitudes (i.e., schemas) rather than specific cognitive errors, attitudes that might once have been functional but that are now less appropriate. An example of such a belief would be a group member who raised 11 children and was active in church and social affairs all her life. Depression emerged when a disability forced her to withdraw from most of her volunteer activities and a move to a new state away from her children. With feedback from therapists and group members, she was able to identify that her distress was caused largely by her belief that her only value as a person lay in the work she was able to do for others. When clients see those schematic assumptions to which they are most subject as basic themes pervading their lives, they can anticipate their most likely reaction to future stress and plan ways to challenge their expected irrational thought patterns ahead of time. Clearly, if one theme is responsible for a significant portion of a person's distress, the management or alteration of that theme will result in a correspondingly large reduction in depression.

MAINTENANCE OF GAINS

At some point during the later sessions of therapy (sessions 15–20), in place of a lecturette, members might be asked to describe the gains they made thus far in the group. After their responses have been listed on the board, leaders can initiate a brainstorming discussion around the question of how to maintain these gains after the group ends, adding any ideas of their own that they believe would be helpful. Typically, group members are able to list many practical and effective ways to handle problem situations and thoughts, such as, (a) avoid times, places, people, and conditions that have elicited depression in the past; (b) seek out people who make you feel good and reward you for being cheerful and for making an effort; (c) refer frequently to a notebook containing hints and plans that you know from experience help you to manage your thoughts; and (d) find a support group other than this one. The following session, participants are given a typewritten copy of the list of suggestions, which can be revised or added to in subsequent sessions as people develop new ways of coping.

There are several other possible maintenance plans. For example, from the earliest sessions, members have been keeping a list of their own cognitions and the rebuttals they find most effective. Leaders can ensure that these lists are kept up-to-date and that members get into the habit of referring to them as a way of coping with depression, emphasizing that this habit will be useful after the end of the group.

During the next to the last session, it is appropriate to provide members with a summary of the cognitive therapy principles and techniques presented in group. Any misunderstandings can be discussed, and members can be asked to identify which particular principles apply most to them and which skills they learned best. The time after group ends can then be presented as an opportunity to practice the skills, with the expectation that doing so will not always completely remove depression. It needs to be stressed that, in time, repeated rehearsal will improve one's skill at countering depression.

Part of the difficulty in maintaining gains arises when a sense of hopelessness overshadows any gains and clients feel that the effort to practice skills might not be worthwhile. One way to address this issue is to ask clients to recall the goals they set for themselves at the beginning of the group and evaluate the progress they made toward these goals. As long as the initial goals were realistic, all clients can be expected to have progressed at least a little. However minimal this progress, it can nevertheless be presented as evidence that the person has indeed made changes and, thus, further change is possible. Clients might be encouraged at this point to set small, attainable goals for themselves for the posttherapy period. This is an especially valuable device if there are to be follow-up sessions, where such goals could be evaluated. Discussing their initial expectation and the actual results of the group treatment helps clients see and retain therapeutic gains.

Of critical importance in this final stage is the inoculation of clients against further stress, which can be accomplished by asking clients to anticipate problems they expect to encounter after the group is over. Each participant might be asked, in turn, to identify a few specific problems or stressors that might occur in the near future and that might affect their depression, including in this list the termination of the group. The person is then asked to describe dysfunctional cognitions that could arise and several ways in which he or she plans to handle these anticipated problems. Other group members can then make additional suggestions for managing or avoiding the particular difficulties. At this point, the focus of intervention is on assisting each individual to define ways of coping with future problems. Clients are encouraged to keep notes on this process for future reference.

SEPARATING FROM THE GROUP

Separation from the group often raises emotional reactions in members. The imminent closing of the group can elicit a variety of feelings in the participants, some of whom may react with a dramatic increase in problem behaviors and depressive symptoms. Indeed, our experience is that symptoms are often exaggerated, nearly to pretreatment levels, just prior to and after the final group sessions. These symptoms pass rapidly, however, and should be addressed as temporary events. Some participants might feel rejected or abandoned by the leaders; others, sad that the relationships are now ending, a sadness that is intensified if termination of the group brings up memories of past separations. Still others might dread the loss of support provided by the group, the extent of this dread often depending on the extent of their social isolation. Although some participants might feel relieved that they have successfully resolved their difficulties and can operate independently now, others will feel anxious about their ability to handle future problems.

Separation issues need to be addressed directly; if these concerns are left to the last session, they are likely to be overwhelming. The issue of termination needs, therefore, to be raised specifically within the last quarter or third of the group. Leaders could, for example, explain common reactions to the termination of a group and ask if any member is experiencing similar reactions. Clients often feel relief in sharing the feelings and discovering that others feel the same way. Once the feelings have been aired and acknowledged as normal and reasonable, they can be approached in one-to-one contact work and investigated for any irrational thoughts (see Table 7.1). If group members are not aware of any cognitions, it might be useful to initiate a group exercise in which participants imagine that the group has ended and are asked what thoughts and feelings this situation evokes.

The development of alternative social support can minimize the impact of the loss of the group. The continuance of social support can be directed either at finding other support systems or at continuing to hold informal gatherings of the group. It is likely that someone in the group will suggest that the members continue to meet after the official end of the group. Leaders should, therefore, discuss this possibility with one another, in advance, in order to be ready to respond to the idea. In particular, the leaders need to decide the extent to which they are willing to be involved

Table 7.1. Cognitive Approach to Loss of Group

A Situation	B Thoughts	C Feelings
Ending of group	I won't be able to make it without group. I'll get depressed again.	Depressed Helpless

Belief
"I need group to fight my depression."

Interventions
1. "What evidence do you have? You haven't tried to go without the group since you've learned about depression."
2. "Are there alternatives to group?"
3. "Group has only taken up 1½–2 hours a week. Look at all you have done during the rest of each week to combat depression."
4. "If Jack (another group member) said he felt unable to cope without group, what would you say to him?"

in any extension of the group. For example, are they willing to act as group leaders? To find the group a meeting place or another leader? To act as occasional consultants? Some of the issues related to social supports can be addressed through lecturettes and homework assignments.

Lecturette: Building Support Networks

Explanation. We all need the support of other human beings, not only in times of crisis, but also in our everyday lives. Unfortunately, the elderly are often without such support, as social networks tend to shrink when people get older. Friends and family die or move away, retirement brings with it an automatic loss of co-workers, and frequently the elderly, themselves, move to nearby retirement communities or even across the country to places with more hospitable climates. In addition, aging tends to increase social isolation because the physical effort to make social contacts becomes increasingly difficult, and many older adults think it takes too much effort.

Although, it is common for the elderly to have diminished social support networks, the situation need not stay that way; lack of social support is a problem to be solved like any other. Social networks can be restored, but to do so a person must make a systematic effort to both maintain old social contacts and establish new ones. This task is not as simple as it may seem, because dysfunctional cognitions often stop people from taking action. They tell themselves that it takes too much effort to make social contacts ("I just don't have the energy any more to entertain") and that they shouldn't have to make such an effort ("If she wanted to see me she'd call me"). They compare new acquaintances with old friends and find the acquaintances wanting, and they fear rejection, believing that they have nothing to offer. For example, illness forced Shirley to move from Michigan to southern Arizona. Upon arrival, she joined several community groups and tried to make friends, but no one she met seemed as much fun as her old friends back home. She wondered, too, why her neighbors didn't drop by to visit. After all, in Michigan, she always welcomed newcomers to the neighborhood, but no one in her new community appeared to have any manners. She began to avoid going out and spent an increasing amount of time alone, with frequent thoughts such as, "No one here cares about me," "They must think I'm not worth bothering with," and "I don't have anything in common with these people." The more she stayed home with these thoughts, the less she felt like going out, and the more isolated she became. Shirley became increasingly depressed and felt trapped, since she disliked the people in Arizona yet could not afford to move back to Michigan.

In another example, family problems over several months took Joe's time away from his usual circle of golfing friends. When he finally had more time, he waited for someone to invite him to play golf and was hurt and angry when this did not happen. He thought, "They've all forgotten me. That's how much they care about me." When someone finally called, Joe was grumpy and brusque and refused the invitation. Like Shirley, Joe missed people and became increasingly depressed.

Personal Application. Therapists should initiate a brief discussion of members' social support networks, focusing mainly on whether the networks are perceived as adequate and on possible options for expansion. If networks have shrunk over the years, there is little point in encouraging much talk about reasons for the loss. Instead, therapists should investigate the barriers, especially cognitive ones, to increasing social support in the present time. Ask, "What is preventing you now from building a new circle of friends?" Usually, the group is very helpful in dealing with practical barriers, such as transportation, and knowledgeable about available activities. Dysfunctional thoughts can be addressed within a cognitive framework (see Table 7.2).

Most of the personal application section of the lecturette should be focused on intervention; that is, on building social support networks. Therapists should assume that the participants already have the requisite skills to establish and maintain social relationships and do not need to be taught. In order to define and plan or expand the network, ask participants the following questions:

1. Who is in your social network now?
2. Do you feel you have enough people in your life?

Table 7.2. Cognitive Approach to Inadequate Social Support

A Situation	B Thoughts	C Feelings
Inadequate social support network	No one will want to be my friend. I have nothing to offer.	Hopelessness Alone

Belief
''People only want to be friends with someone young, active, rich, attractive, etc.''

Interventions
1. ''You have had friends in the past. What qualities did they like you for that you still possess?''
2. ''What is the evidence for your belief? Has everyone refused your friendship? How do you account for friendships among people who are *not* young, rich, etc.?''
3. ''Are your expectations realistic? How quickly do you expect a friendship to develop? Do you expect the relationship to develop without any problems?''
4. ''How are you defining *friend*? Would you be more successful if you tried, for acquaintances or casual friendship first?''

3. What acquaintances do you have who could conceivably be friends?
4. How might you go about strengthening your relationships with these people?
5. Or, if there are no acquaintances who could be friends, how and where could you meet people?

Homework. In order to build a social support network, you must be active in initiating and maintaining friendships; you cannot build a support network by waiting for other people to come to you.

Identify two occasions over the next week in which you could either take the initiative to meet someone new or extend an invitation to someone whom you already know but haven't seen recently. Specifically, how, when, and where you will take these steps?

THE FINAL SESSION

If leaders remain sensitive to the needs and responses of the group members, and build in the termination process from the start of the group, the final session should entail a minimum of disappointment and panic. The actual content and format of this last meeting is usually determined by the leaders' perceptions of any final business that needs attention and by the decision of the members. The extended number of sessions recommended for older adults and the inclusion of social time each week usually results in the formation of friendships, or at least social relationships among the members, who frequently enjoy turning at least a portion of the last meeting into a social occasion, for example, lunching together.

If such is the wish of the group, the agenda for the last session might well need to be planned at the previous meeting.

However flexible this final session, leaders should attempt to meet several goals: as far as possible, no one should have any serious unfinished business; group members should leave on a positive note, conscious of gains made and skills acquired; no one should feel abandoned, with no place to turn for help. Resulting from these goals, a possible agenda for the last session might contain (a) any unfinished business; (b) quick review of methods for handling problems; (c) a round where both leaders and other members describe changes that they have seen each member make in the course of therapy; and (d) referral sources.

Chapter 8
The Art of Group Cognitive Therapy with Older Adults

In previous chapters, we tried to simplify and distill cognitive therapy into a step-by-step approach that could be easily understood and put into practice. Such simplification has made it necessary, however, to deemphasize those subtle aspects of therapy that are important to all successful therapeutic ventures. These fine nuances elevate therapy to an art rather than just a collection of techniques applied in a routine and mechanical way. In all art, much of success is due to the effective blending and balancing of diverse and, seemingly, unrelated elements. In the case of group cognitive therapy, the art lies in balancing the sometimes mutually exclusive needs and competing characteristics of four systems: cognitive therapy, the group, the leaders, and the individual members. One might, therefore, examine the interactions in the group, together with the needs that prompt these interactions and the rules that govern them, in order to discern the extent to which the four systems are in balance. As a result of this examination, therapists can—indeed they must—develop interventions to correct any imbalance. Failure to do so is likely to produce such serious negative effects as increased client dropout, decreased client satisfaction, and reduced treatment efficacy.

The particular combination of (a) the individual needs of group members, (b) the tasks of cognitive therapy, (c) the demands and needs imposed by group norms, and (d) the goals of leaders, who are in all likelihood much younger than the group members, produces some highly specific concerns that need to be addressed. In this chapter we examine ways in which the specific needs of the four systems can disturb the healing process of the group and disrupt the task of producing change. We also discuss methods of dealing with the conflicting needs of all concerned, so as to maximize the effect of therapy.

INDIVIDUAL NEEDS

Clients enter the group with emotional needs that can either facilitate or interfere with therapy. Because of the specificity of the cognitive approach, at times an individual's needs will conflict with the needs of the group or of the approach. When a balance is not struck, members can view the group leaders as ineffective, insensitive, or uncaring. These negative perceptions will inevitably interfere with therapy.

Probably, the first problem likely to upset the balance in a group occurs when a particular member requires a great deal of *attention*. The need becomes apparent when a client consistently is the focus of the group interactions. The client might monopolize time when asked a question or refocus the group on his or her own material, while ostensibly attempting to support another member. The personal material introduced may or may not be pertinent to the day's agenda. Regardless of the value of the contribution, demands for attention are a problem when the therapist or other group members become irritated with the individual or when agenda items are neglected due to lack of time. This problem is difficult to address directly, since the individual needing attention will often insist that the comments are relevant, are attempts at self-disclosure, or are to help others. If one or two clients are allowed to dominate and monopolize group time, the leaders will be viewed as ineffective and will, in fact, be unable to meet the requirements of cognitive therapy. A technique that has proven useful is simply to interrupt the client's discourse with comments such as, "That sounds like an important point. I wonder if you would summarize it for us," or "It sounds as if that's an important issue for you. Unfortunately, our time is limited and I wonder if you would be willing to place it on the agenda next week." If this refocusing is done in a sensitive manner, the client returns to the topic at hand and the therapist continues to be seen as effective and caring.

A second need members might have is for emotion-expression or catharsis. Since many clients have never before discussed with others the painful topics they raise in the group, they often need to spend a great deal of time, perhaps on several different occasions, describing just how bad a situation was. This release of emotion becomes a problem under two conditions: when the lengthy, repeated discussion of the negative situation does not produce changes in the clients' affect, cognitions, or behavior and consumes group time without employing cognitive therapy principles, or when a cathartic experience is of value to the client, in that emotional intensity diminishes over time after repetition, but greatly diminishes the time available for cognitive therapy or for other members.

These two conditions need to be addressed in different ways. With those who are, in essence, wallowing in unproductive emotionality, therapists can respond, first, with an empathic statement to indicate understanding of the person's pain and, second, with a request to focus on change. For example, "Your situation and hiding it for years must have been terribly difficult for you. Would you be willing to look at some ways to change your response to the situation?" To help the client realize that the feelings are understood but the focus must turn to changing cognitions, another group member could be asked to summarize what has been said, then ask the first client what needs to be added before going on to identifying or changing thoughts. When it is apparent that repeated and prolonged visitation is therapeutic for the client, therapists might reconsider the client's appropriateness for group in view of time considerations.

The *multiple problems* that clients have must be balanced against the cognitive therapy format of focusing on one problem at a time. The elderly, in particular, often enter therapy with a number of serious issues, all of which they hope will be resolved as soon as possible. Often, during contact work, while the therapist works toward cognitive change on one problem, the client switches to a different issue, and contact work is stymied. A possible way to handle this problem is for the therapist and client to agree to a specific focus for contact work before the work begins. Then when a switch occurs, the therapist can remind the client of the original contract and suggest putting the second problem on hold.

The issue of multiple problems can also arise when the therapist has planned an intervention involving several weeks of in-session work and homework assignments. Before this work is completed, an urgent new problem occurs in the client's life, threatening to displace in importance the previous problem. If the therapist, in an attempt to maintain the focus on the original problem, tries to work with both problems, the client might feel overwhelmed. On the other hand, a therapist who tries to downplay the new problem might be seen as unresponsive to the new concern. The resolution of this issue requires that both therapist and client negotiate the goals of therapy. The therapist might tell the client, "I recognize that this new concern is very distressing for you, but we need to decide which problem to work on, the new one or the old. You've been making progress on the old problem, and have put a lot of time and effort into it, so you might be reluctant to abandon it. On the other hand, you may feel that this new problem is too important to ignore. What do you think?"

Sometimes older adults bring to the group strong *dependency needs*, which can manifest themselves as an expectation that the leaders will take responsibility for the member's problems. It is often difficult for dependent clients to commit time and energy to homework assignments or to take an active problem-solving stance during sessions. Their dependency needs conflict with the emphasis of cognitive therapy on a more egalitarian, collaborative relationship between therapist and client. If the therapist assumes too active a role, the client is unable to apply in-session learning outside the group. Several strategies can be effective with dependent clients. The therapist can make the conflict explicit by explaining the client-therapist roles appropriate to cognitive therapy, then deal with the client's underlying theme of helplessness (see Table 8.1). It can also be helpful to transfer the dependency from the therapist to a larger audience by asking the client to enlist the help of others, both within the group and outside, to help solve a particular problem. Finally, such clients can be encouraged to offer help and advice to others in the group, in the hope that evidence of their ability to help others will counteract a sense of dependent helplessness.

DEMAND CHARACTERISTICS OF COGNITIVE THERAPY

The specificity of the cognitive approach dictates a certain structure that the therapist must balance with needs of the individual and the group. Ignoring this structure reduces the effectiveness of the therapy, yet too strict an adherence to protocol can result in the mechanical administration of a program that fails to respond to individual needs.

Three major problems can arise when therapists conduct cognitive therapy: some group members might fail to understand the basic concepts of this approach; even when understanding exists, some people might disagree with the attribution of depression to internal events; and, at times, individual problems require reference to concepts not yet taught.

A basic requirement of cognitive therapy is that clients *understand the conceptual framework of the approach* in order to complete homework assign-

Table 8.1. Cognitive Approach to Dependency Needs

A Situation	B Thoughts	C Feelings
Homework assignment	I can't do this on my own. They don't understand how difficult that sounds to me.	Helpless Angry

Belief
"I'm incapable of doing things on my own. Others should help me."

Interventions
1. "What evidence do you have that you can't do things on your own in situations when you've genuinely tried?"
2. "Can you design a step-by-step program that would allow you to complete the assignment?" (Once accomplished, this constitutes evidence of capability.)

ments and institute strategies for change. Some clients, however, fail to grasp what is being discussed. They might do homework assignments in a fashion that indicates they either do not understand the approach or cannot apply it without the therapist supporting them each step of the way. While this lack of understanding can be frustrating to the therapist, who might consider dropping the client from group, it is not necessarily a sign that the treatment should be terminated. Often the therapeutic factors of groups (as discussed in Chapter 2) have a positive impact on the individual and lead to improvement in depressive symptoms. In addition, the loss of a group member can be upsetting to the rest of the group. Referral out of the group would probably be indicated only if the client's distress at failing to comprehend the material outweighed the gains from group participation.

The focus of cognitive therapy on self-governed cognitions occasionally conflicts with the external *attributions of feelings* that clients have maintained over the years. Clients might contend that the depressive quality in a given situation is due to forces out of their control, and this is often the case, at least in part. A client might maintain, for example, ''My depression is the result of my failing eyesight, which means I can't get around or do much anymore.'' When the therapist accepts this explanation for depression, however, change becomes impossible and both therapist and client are left feeling overwhelmed and helpless. Change is possible only if the situation is reevaluated and reframed according to self-controlled cognitions rather than blamed on external events. Therapists need to monitor their own reactions to clients' explanations of depression and note a sense of helplessness or an inclination to think ''I'd be depressed, too.'' Such reactions signal the need to focus on exploring cognitions rather than the external factors of the situation. This move can be accomplished by the therapists' acknowledgement that the situation is indeed distressing, and that since little or nothing can be done about the circumstances, it is important to examine cognitions. The balance to be struck in this therapeutic endeavor is between the power of external forces and the power of the individuals to change their own cognitions. Falling too exclusively within either the cognitive or the environmental explanation can result in difficulty. On the one hand, accepting external explanations leads to a sense of helplessness for both client and therapist. On the other hand, focusing exclusively on the power of the client to resolve the depressive situation by cognitive changes might be interpreted by the client as the therapist's lack of sympathy. A balance between these two interpretations can often be struck by asking the client to temporarily hold in check his or her explanation while the two of you examine other possible influences in the depressing situation.

A third requirement of cognitive therapy is the *step-by-step development* of the underlying conceptual framework. Occasionally, clients will identify situations or cognitions that most clearly fit with material not yet covered in the weekly lecturettes. For example, a client might present an excellent example of catastrophizing before this style of cognitive error has been presented. Three options present themselves in balancing the need to take a step-by-step approach and the need to address the problem at hand. The first option is to ask the client if this situation could be put on hold until the necessary topic is covered. The second option is to present the needed material out of the planned sequence. Third, since most problems are accompanied by more than one cognitive error, the therapist can help the client to identify a different error already familiar to the group. It must be left to the therapist's clinical judgment to choose which option best suits the situation.

GROUP NORMS

In addition to the needs of individuals and the structure of the therapy, group norms constitute a third system that can upset the balance of therapy. Group norms can be defined as the rules that govern interactions within the group. According to research, a group's success depends in part on its ability to maintain a set of norms that differ from those of society at large (Lieberman, Yalom, & Miles, 1973). This condition is difficult to meet in groups composed of a single client population, since one effect of group homogeneity is that a majority of the participants bring a common set of behavioral rules into group. With the elderly, many of the expectations of behavior are in conflict with the goals or techniques of the therapist. As we list examples of norms that have emerged in our cognitive therapy groups, it is important to note that this list is not exhaustive, nor do we imply that these norms are held by all elderly clients or even by all groups. Since these and similar norms often represent lifetime values, clients might persist in endorsing the beliefs and refuse to see them as dysfunctional. Therapists should, therefore, approach these norms with respect and sensitivity.

A very prominent behavioral norm brought to group by older adults is that *"one should not air dirty laundry in public."* This norm tends to constrain the group members' willingness to share personal material. Even though the issue of self-disclosure was raised both in the pre-induction interview and probably in the first group session, it might still influence the behavior of individual group members. One way this issue can be resolved is by making it explicit when it seems to be limiting an individual's contribution. Contact work centered on this norm is most likely to be useful when a client raises issues but consistently declines to spend additional time on them. In such a situation, the therapist might comment,

The Art of Group Cognitive Therapy

for example, ''I notice that you often raise problems in group but have not yet added them to the agenda for further exploration. I wonder if you have any thoughts or feelings that make it difficult for you to talk in detail about these matters in the group?'' Once the client's concerns are explicit, the therapist can often address them within a cognitive therapy framework; for example, by using group experiments to test dysfunctional cognitions around such issues as being judged by others, being ashamed, being socially unacceptable—all of which can arise from the ''dirty laundry'' rule (see Table 8.2).

''*Don't express emotions*'' is another social rule that can interfere with therapy. While excessive amounts of emotional stimulation may not be desirable in group therapy (Lieberman et al., 1973), it is often useful for clients to re-experience the emotional aspects of situations in order to identify cognitions. It is thus apparent that a prohibition on emotional expression can interfere with therapy. Once again, when the rule is made explicit it offers clinical material that can be addressed as dysfunctional cognitions (see Table 8.3).

Rules of behavior about *politeness* constitute another set of norms to which elderly clients often adhere and that may interfere with therapy. Being polite often translates into not disagreeing with the therapist and not commenting on another's behavior. Adherence to these rules interferes with giving feedback if, for example, members are reluctant to tell the therapist when an intervention is not helpful or to tell another group member that his or her thoughts seem dysfunctional. Once again, if the unstated rule that limits behavior can be made explicit, it can be evaluated within a cognitive framework, and the members can formulate a definition of rudeness that will serve the purposes of the group (see Table 8.4). It may even be possible, for example, to establish that such behaviors as disagreeing, commenting on another's thinking, or probing are helpful rather than impolite.

Table 8.2. Cognitive Approach to "Dirty Laundry" Rule

A Situation	B Thoughts	C Feelings
Time to add items to the agenda	I must not talk about this problem. others will think less of me.	Isolated, ashamed

Belief
"One must not raise problems in public."

Interventions
1. "Do you have any evidence for the thought that others will think less of you?"
2. "Can you ask other members what they would think if you introduced problems?"

Table 8.3. Cognitive Approach to "Don't Express Emotion" Rule

A Situation	B Thoughts	C Feelings
Issue raised, feelings stirred	If I cry, others will think I'm weak. If I start crying, I won't be able to stop.	Ashamed Scared

Belief
"Emotions are overwhelming and must be controlled."

Interventions
1. "Can you check out with others what they would think if you cried?"
2. "What evidence do you have that once you begin crying it will go on forever." (If they raise a time when they did cry at length, point out that they were able to pull themselves together eventually.)

Establishment of Norms

Our experience is that when appropriate behavior in groups is initially discussed, few questions arise. Once the group has met several times, however, questions begin to emerge such as, "What are we to talk about here?" or "Is it all right to talk out of turn?" Frequently, this occurs when members are caught between group norms and social norms. For example, one member wished to know if it would be acceptable to discuss her negative feelings about her deceased husband. She was torn between a lifelong norm dictating loyalty to one's spouse and the group norm of discussing distressing concerns. Another example occurred when a man's social norm, that people should not be made to experience painful emotions, conflicted with the group norm that required exploration of uncomfortable memories. His efforts to rescue a member in distress from the

Table 8.4. Cognitive Approach to "I Must be Polite" Rule

A Situation	B Thoughts	C Feelings
Time to give feedback	I should not disagree with the therapist. I should not comment on others' problems if I have my own.	Conflict over whether to say things. Distant from others.

Belief
"I must be polite and not disagree or make comments about others."

Interventions
1. "What evidence do you have that others will see you as impolite?"
2. "Is politeness more important than helping yourself or others?"

probing of the therapist resulted in a discussion of the norm of emotional questioning.

The following dialogue is based on a group discussion in which the therapist attempted to help an individual client, and the group as a whole, explore appropriate group behavior around the topic of what issues should be discussed in group. In the interests of clarity, the conversation has been condensed to retain only relevant material. The actual discussion was not quite as highly focused.

Client 1: I just was wondering what topics are appropriate to raise in group.

Therapist: Do you have specific topics you aren't sure about?

Client 1: Well, I have some difficulties when I think about my husband before he died.

Therapist: And what makes you question the appropriateness of these difficulties for group?

Client 1: I don't know. I'm just not sure the others would want to hear about my problems from the past.

Therapist: Centered around this topic of your husband, I hear two important questions, one a general one of what is appropriate to raise in the groups and a second as to whether you want to raise the specific issue of your husband.

Client 1: Yes.

Therapist: Would you be willing to let the group in general address the general question of appropriate topics for group, then decide whether you want to raise the issue of your husband?

Client 1: Yes.

Therapist: Good. Then let me throw the question out to the group as a whole. What topics are appropriate for group?

Client 2: Well, I think anything that anybody wants to talk about is fine.

Client 3: Sure, anything that is bothering anyone is legitimate for group. Listening to the others talk helps me learn regardless of what the topic is.

Therapist: Well that's great. It's nice to hear that you're so willing to listen. But what about as speakers, how do you all decide what issues to raise?

(No response from any client.)

Therapist: Maybe by looking at this in ABC terms will be helpful. Let's look

124 Group Cognitive Therapy

at two alternative situations: one is the decision to raise a sensitive issue and another is the decision not to raise a sensitive issue. Let me list the feelings that might contribute to each of these decisions on the board under the C column. What feelings would cause each of you not to raise an issue?

Client 2: The feeling that others weren't interested.

Therapist: That is really more of an interpretation of others' feelings. So I'll list it in the B column. What about your feelings in that situation?

Client 2: Well, if I thought others weren't interested I'd feel like I was boring or dull.

Therapist: Good. That fits more with what should go in our C column. Boring or dull. How about unimportant? Does that fit with the idea that others aren't interested?

Client 2: Yes it does.

Client 4: How about scared?

Therapist: That sounds like something that would keep people from talking. Can you elaborate on that a little so we can develop the thought behind the scare?

Client 4: Well, I don't know. Sometimes I feel that if I open my mouth it won't come out right, so I just don't say anything.

Client 1: Another scary thing you might say to yourself is that what you have to say may shock others.

Therapist: I know both of those types of scare would prevent me from talking. Any other feelings that might stop folks?

Client 3: Being embarrassed about the situation, thinking others might judge you.

Therapist: Good. Any others? . . . Now let's look at the feelings that might prompt people to decide to raise an issue.

Client 3: Well it just seems it would be the opposite of all the feelings you've just written.

Therapist: Specifically?

Client 3: Well, feeling that others are interested and that you're important. Feeling that you are safe and that you can express yourself and that others won't be shocked. And, finally, not having to feel embarrassed about the past.

Therapist: That sounds like a pretty big order. Do people feel that it would make a difference whether a person decides to raise a problem or not?

Client 1: Well, it seems to me for someone to get the most out of group they'd have to raise problems.

Client 2: Yes. I'd hate to think people could not talk because they thought I might be shocked.

Therapist: Now, I would like to return to the situation concerning your husband and ask if you felt any of these feelings we've discussed and whether they caused you to raise the issue of appropriateness of the topic.

Client 1: Well, two of them I guess. I've been telling myself that others wouldn't be interested and that they might think badly of me.

Therapist: Can you tell which situations prompted these thoughts, what A's?

Client 1: Well, the last couple of times I talked Mary shifted in her chair a lot and seemed uninterested. And then I also worried about what Sally might think if I talked about problems with my husband after she's sounded so devoted to hers.

Therapist: Could you try an experiment here and test out your cognitions by asking each of those people?

Client 1: Well, Sally, would you think less of me if I talked about problems with my husband?

Client 2: Heavens no! My husband and I went through our share of problems. I guess I never mentioned them because I didn't want people to feel I wasn't a good wife.

Client 3: And I'd just like to say that the reason I've been shifting around a lot is that these chairs are uncomfortable and my arthritis is bothering me. I've always found the things you said very interesting.

Therapist: Well, do the results influence your interpretation and feelings about the situation?

Client 1: Yes, I guess it does. And I think it might do me good to talk about my husband.

Therapist: Before you go on, I'd just like to point out that during the time we are all in group it will be important to discuss the thoughts and feelings that influence our behavior here. I think discussing feelings about group allows us to use experiments and make decisions here that will be important to our discussion and may even carry over into our life outside group.

LEADERSHIP ISSUES

Group leaders play a double part in the success of therapy. In the sense that they have their own reactions and needs, they represent a fourth system to be balanced with the group, the individual, and the therapy. The leaders are also, however, the artists who must stand apart from the process and actively perform the balancing act. In order to respond adequately to this challenge—that is, to practice the art of group cognitive therapy— it is clearly important that leaders retain the objectivity and emotional distance required for such a function. But certain aspects of conducting group cognitive therapy with depressed older adults have the potential to reduce the leaders' ability to fully manage their leadership task. In this section, we discuss the impact on the leaders, and therefore ultimately on the success of therapy, of such factors as age differences between leaders and members, the leaders' own family relationships, multiple role demands, the mood of the group, the leaders' own dysfunctional cognitions, and the use of cotherapists.

The single most obvious difference between group members and leaders is usually their ages. In general, therapists are likely to be 20, 30, even as much as 50 years younger than their clients. This alone creates an instant gap in credibility and empathy. A person in the prime of life, in the middle of a busy and very likely successful career, and in possession of a body that still functions more or less as expected has experienced neither the developmental stages of later life nor most of the problems that concern older people. In a real sense, then, therapists cannot understand what it is like to be old, and this reality can create difficulties that take time and energy away from therapeutic tasks. We consider some of these difficulties, their impact on therapy, and suggest some ways to deal with them.

Failure to Empathize

Frequently, the leaders will have to contend with the accusation that they do not understand the concerns of the elderly and, therefore, cannot be of help. A belief such as this sabotages therapy from the start, since some people are unwilling to make a commitment to therapy when it appears to them that there is no hope of help. Other members will take up group time in repeated efforts to convince the young therapists how difficult it is to be old. Still others will use the age difference as a reason to discount therapeutic interventions. Since this particular aspect of age difference arises so frequently, we recommend that leaders working with groups significantly older than themselves air it in the first session, even before it has been vocalized by members. We found it effective for therapists to admit that lack of experience of various problems does limit understanding, but that the client who is experiencing the problems is in a position to teach the therapists what needs to be known to allow the therapists to design appropriate interventions. If clients continue to attach importance to the age disparity, the belief and its accompanying negative feelings can be addressed in a cognitive framework (see Table 8.5).

Interpersonal Style

Generation differences can be apparent in therapists' and members' interpersonal styles. Typically, older people prefer quite formal social manners and speech and might object to swearing, slang, jokes about sex or religion, and the use of first names on first acquaintance. While a warm handshake at the start and end of each session is appreciated, an embrace, however well intended, might not be viewed as appropriate. The tone of a therapist's voice is also important. An effort to be audible to members with hearing problems and to instill some energy into the session can easily sound strident and jarring, as if you are talking to people you believe to be unintelligent. When leaders' interpersonal style is offensive to clients due to generational differences, clients can develop negative cognitions about leaders' politeness, sensitivity, suitability for the leadership role, etc., which can have a negative effect on therapy. A review of video- or audio-tapes of the sessions is an excellent way for leaders to monitor both the manner in which they address participants and the response of group members to the leaders.

Table 8.5. Cognitive Approach to Therapist-Client Age Difference

A Situation	B Thoughts	C Feelings
Age difference	Leader can't help being too young to understand my problems.	Hopeless Not interested Giving up

Belief
"Only people the same age can understand one another."

Interventions
1. "Do you have to be totally understood in order for someone to help you?"
2. "Is it important for understanding that someone experience the same situation or the same sorts of feelings?"
3. "Is being the same age and in the same situation a guarantee that you are understood and can be helped by that person, or are there other requirements of helpers, which younger people could meet?"

Parent-Child Roles

The gap in years often causes therapists to respond to group members as they would to their own parents. As a result, when members complain about their children, a leader who is currently experiencing a similar difficulty might find it hard to remain objective. In such a situation, leaders might behave in a variety of unproductive ways: they might avoid interaction with the member; they might focus on their own negative emotions toward their parents; or they might attempt to justify the behavior of the younger generation. Since such emotional involvement is unlikely to be therapeutic for the group, it should be avoided as far as possible.

We can suggest some ways to achieve a reasonable objectivity on this issue of role contamination, the most important probably being to maintain an awareness that the problem can and does exist. The leaders should review each session, as soon as possible after its occurrence, and systematically examine their own emotional reactions to and interactions with the participants. If one member in particular seems to arouse strong reactions in one of the leaders, the other leader can agree to take on the major therapeutic work with that member. Another focus of the session review can be to examine whether the leaders are allowing themselves to slip out of the role of leader into that of a child. This awareness can be used to help the therapists plan how to respond differently in ensuing sessions. Since one characteristic of the parent-child relationship is differential authority, leaders should also check to see that they are not passively accepting the older adults' view of problem situations and ignoring any cognitive distortions.

Therapist Cognitions

Another leadership issue we must address is the therapists' development of their own negative cognitions. One area of difficulty for leaders arises from the negative content of many sessions. Every group of depressed clients discusses unhappy events and upsetting emotions, but the elderly are far more likely to focus on loss, degeneration, and death. In the course of a group a member might receive diagnosis of a terminal illness, be permanently hospitalized, or even die. Since close relationships often form between leaders and members, this sort of event can be upsetting to the leaders, who find themselves also becoming depressed.

Depressive cognitions also tend to develop around the question of physical health. Leaders' cognitions on this topic might center on the utility of psychotherapy when medical problems are so overwhelming. In addition, leaders might come to dwell on the fact that someday they, themselves, could be in the same position as the members they are trying to help: old, sick, poor, depressed. As might be expected, negative cognitions and feelings of depression lead to feelings of hopelessness and helplessness that interfere with therapists' effectiveness in the group. Once a therapist recognizes that depression is developing in connection with the group, it might be best to consult with the cotherapist, with supervisors, or with colleagues, in order to explore the problem within a cognitive framework. In Table 8.6 we suggest such an approach.

The slow rate of progress, often typical with depressed older adults, can be discouraging to leaders. Therapy can be slowed by clients' cognitive deficits, intervening traumatic events, and environmental obstacles. Typically, leaders tend to start entertaining such thoughts as, "I'm not doing a good job as leader" or "These people have made no progress and probably aren't going to." These depressive self-doubts and gloomy predictions are bound to be communicated to group members, who are inclined to believe them and to become further discouraged. Once again, the therapist might be advised to consult others and to pursue a cognitive approach to the dysfunctional cognitions (see Table 8.7).

It is possible for therapists to develop many different negative cognitions. We mentioned just two in order to illustrate the kinds of reactions possible. The need is obvious for cotherapists to monitor their individual and shared cognitions about the group, specifically, and about aging, more generally. Once negative cognitions are recognized, they can be altered in the manner we have suggested. Various writers (Altholz, 1978; Corey & Corey, 1982; Goldfarb, 1971; Yost & Corbishley, 1985) have recommended several ways to prevent the negative cognitions that can arise when therapists work with the elderly. They suggest, for example, that thera-

Table 8.6. Cognitive Approach to Therapist Cognitions of Aging

A Situation	B Thoughts	C Feelings
Medical problems in members	Therapy's no good for these people— they're too ill. I dread getting old— it's a terrible time of life.	Helpless, useless

Belief
"You have to be young and healthy to enjoy life. Nothing helps if you're not."

Interventions
1. "Are there no exceptions to this belief; for example, do you know any older people in poor health who are still happy?"
2. "How much do they have to improve to make it worthwhile for you to work together? Isn't any change for the better worth your trouble?"
3. "Is being young and healthy a guarantee that you'll enjoy life or are there other factors, accessible to old sick people?"

Table 8.7. Cognitive Approach to Therapist Discouragement

A Situation	B Thoughts	C Feelings
Slow or minimal progress of clients in therapy	I'm no good as a leader.	Discouraged Incompetent

Belief
"If I'm an effective leader, all group members will make considerable and rapid progress."

Interventions
1. "How much of your client's progress are you responsible for? What responsibility does your cotherapist share in this situation?
2. "Would you apply this standard to other therapists working with this group?"
3. "How are you measuring progress? Is there another way to look at progress?"

pists not work fulltime with this population and consult regularly with colleagues or supervisors, whose objectivity allows them to both recognize therapist burnout and to evaluate client progress.

Cotherapy Issues

There are certain advantages to conducting group cognitive therapy with a team of cotherapists. First, it rapidly becomes apparent that not all clients respond well to the same therapist. Cotherapists often adjust their roles to accommodate these variations and to maximize the value of the compatible attachments that often develop between a given client and one or another therapist. Second, since portions of the therapy are conducted in client-therapist dyads, the use of cotherapists allows one member of the team to observe the other group members and note reactions that need attention. Third, the use of cotherapists allows the flexibility and creativity of both to come to bear on difficult therapeutic problems.

In spite of these advantages, the process of working with a cotherapist is not easy. Cotherapists must be familiar with each others' working patterns and preferences and must be willing to accommodate differing methods. It is advantageous, therefore, if prospective cotherapists have the opportunity to observe one another in group therapy before actually working together. It is also advantageous for cotherapists to plan their various roles in advance of each session and to have ample opportunity to review the group experience at the end of each session. It is helpful to videotape the group sessions and to utilize outside consultants, from time to time, in order to review group and cotherapy transactions. This is a particularly important recommendation when cotherapists observe that they are not working toward the same objectives or feel frustrated or angry in their interactions with one another.

Three possible roles are available for structuring the interrelationships of cotherapists in group cognitive therapy. The first involves identifying one of the cotherapists as the group leader and assigning to the other cotherapist the role of observer. The leader then becomes responsible for deciding the focus of the group and determines when topics will be changed, activities will be implemented, and the agenda will be discarded. The observer is responsible for noting the group process and bringing to the leader's attention group and interpersonal dynamics that need to be addressed. This method of role structuring is most advantageous when one cotherapist is highly experienced and the other is not or when one cotherapist is just learning to function as a cognitive therapy group leader.

A second method of structuring roles is for the leaders to alternate leader and observer roles from group session to group session. This method of structuring works best when both cotherapists are equally experienced but are unfamiliar with each others' leadership styles. In this method, roles are maximally structured, causing less role confusion and conflict than if both were allowed to develop their own roles in each session. It is not surprising, therefore, that we recommend this method of role structuring when conflicts arise between cotherapists.

The third method of role structuring is to identify, in advance of each group session, which cotherapist will be responsible for each activity. For example, therapist A sets the agenda and reviews homework while therapist B leads the contact work and lecturettes, then therapist A again leads the group discussion that follows each of these activities. As in the previous methods, the therapist who is not assigned the role of leader for a given activity is assigned the role of observer. It is advantageous, therefore, if the observer becomes the group process leader after lecturettes and contact work. This procedure is recommended because the role of observer allows sensitivity to group process activities denied a leader, who is focusing on presenting specific content or a single client. Nonetheless, this third type of leadership role structuring is not recommended until leaders are quite familiar with each others' leadership styles and methods of working. Only when such familiarity is accompanied by respect and patience can alternation of roles work effectively.

Occasionally, leaders who are very familiar with one another and very flexible in their working styles can develop roles that do not require formal structuring. If such cotherapists can learn to read each others' activities very well, the continuity of the group process and instructional activities may not be lost. Since group cognitive therapy is quite highly structured, however, this kind of spontaneous role structuring is not as easy to develop as it is in a process or an experientially oriented group.

FINAL NOTE

In conclusion, it is important to point out, after outlining such a highly structured and specific program, that there are few right or wrong ways to do therapy. Interventions are best evaluated as either more or less productive. We found in our work with depressed older adults that cognitive therapy in groups has been useful and, therefore, hope that this book helps therapists adopt the framework in their clinical practices. However, we also encourage clinicians to explore methods not presented here rather than being content with just a single approach to helping depressed older adults.

In addition to communicating the specifics of a therapeutic program, we hope that we have communicated our own commitment to improving the quality of life for older adults. While the medical establishment has emphasized the extension of life, the quality of those extra years of life, by and large, has been ignored. It is our hope that readers of this book will gain an understanding of the problems faced by older adults, a realization that improvement is possible, and a commitment to work with this population.

References

Altholz, J. A. S. (1978). Group psychotherapy with the elderly. In I. M. Burnside (Ed.), *Working with the elderly: Group process and techniques.* North Scituate, MA: Duxbury.

Anderson, M. P. (1980). Imaginal processes: Therapeutic applications and theoretical models. In M. J. Mahoney (Ed.), *Psychotherapy process* (pp. 211–248). New York: Plenum.

Barnes, R., Veith, R. C., & Raskind, M. A. (1981). Depression in older patients: Diagnosis and management. *Western Journal of Medicine, 135,* 463.

Bates, M., Johnson, C., & Bloaker, K. E. (1982). *Group leadership: A manual for group counseling leaders* (2d ed.). Denver, CO: Love.

Beck, A. T., & Greenberg, R. L. (1974). *Coping with depression.* New York: Institute for Rational Living.

Beck, A. T., Hollon, S. D., Young, J. E., Bedrosian, R. C., & Budenz, D. (1984). Treatment of depression with cognitive therapy and amitriptyline. *Archives of General Psychiatry, 42,* 142–152.

Beck, A. T., Rush, A. J., Shaw, B. F., & Emery, G. (1979). *Cognitive therapy of depression.* New York: Guilford Press.

Beutler, L. E. (1979). Toward specific psychological therapies for specific conditions. *Journal of Consulting and Clinical Psychology, 47,* 882–897.

Beutler, L. E. (1983). *Eclectic psychotherapy: A systematic approach.* New York: Pergamon.

Beutler, L. E. (in press). Systematic eclectic psychotherapy. In J. C. Norcross (Ed.), *Handbook of eclectic psychotherapy.* New York: Brunner/Mazel.

Beutler, L. E., Crago, M., & Arizmendi, T. G. (in press). Therapist variables in psychotherapy process and outcome. In S. L. Garfield & A. E. Bergin (Eds.), *Handbook of psychotherapy and behavior change* (3d ed.). New York: John Wiley and Sons.

Brehm, S. S., & Brehm, J. W. (1981). *Psychological reactance: A theory of freedom and control.* New York: Academic Press.

Bunch, J. (1972). Recent bereavement in relation to suicide. *Journal of Psychosomatic Research, 16,* 361–366.

Busse, E. W. (1978). The Duke longitudinal study: I. Sensescence and senility. In R. Katzman, R. Terry, & K. Bick (Eds.), *Alzheimer's disease: Senile dementia and related disorders.* New York: Raven Press.

Cerella, J., Poon, L. W., & Williams, D. M. (1980). Age and the complexity hypothesis. In L. W. Poon (Ed.), *Aging in the 1980's: Psychological issues* (pp. 332–342). Washington, DC: American Psychological Association.

Chaisson, G. M., Beutler, L. E., Yost, E. B., & Allender, J. (1984). Treating the depressed elderly. *Journal of Psychosocial Nursing, 22,* 25–30.

Chaisson-Stewart, G. M. (1985). Depression incidence: Past, present, and future. In G. M. Chaisson-Stewart (Ed.), *Depression in the elderly: An interdisciplinary approach.* New York: John Wiley and Sons.

Chapron, D., & Lawson, I. (1978). Drug prescribing and care of the elderly. In W. Reichel (Ed.), *Clinical aspects of aging* (pp. 13-32). Baltimore: Williams & Wilkins.

Clayton, P. J. (1974). Mortality and morbidity in the first year of widowhood. *Archives of General Psychiatry, 30,* 747-750.

Clayton, P. J. (1979). The sequalae and nonsequalae of conjugal bereavement. *American Journal of Psychiatry, 136,* 1530-1534.

Clayton, P. J., Halikas, J. A., & Maurice, W. L. (1972). The depression of widowhood. *British Journal of Psychiatry, 120,* 71-78.

Commerford, K. A. (1984). Communication in the doctor-patient relationship: Perceptions of the older adult. (Doctoral dissertation, University of Arizona, 1984). *Dissertation Abstracts International, 45,* 3466B.

Corey, G., & Corey, M. S. (1982). *Groups: Process and practice* (2d ed.). Monterey, CA: Brooks/Cole.

Covi, L., Roth, D., & Lipman, R. S. (1982). Cognitive group psychotherapy of depression: The close-ended group. *American Journal of Psychotherapy, 36,* 459-469.

Cox, P. R., & Ford, J. R. (1967). The mortality of widows shortly after widowhood. *Lancet, 1,* 163-164.

Coyne, J. C., & Gotlib, I. H. (1983). The role of cognition in depression: A critical appraisal. *Psychological Bulletin, 94,* 472-505.

Deutsch, C. B., & Kramer, N. (1977). Outpatient group psychotherapy for the elderly: An alternative to institutionalization. *Hospital and Community Psychiatry, 28,* 440-442.

Dovenmuele, R. H., & Vervoerdt, A. (1962). Physical illness and depressive symptomatology. *Journal of the American Geriatric Society, 10,* 932-947.

Eaves, G., & Rush, A. J. (1984). Cognitive patterns in symptomatic and remitted unipolar depression. *Journal of Abnormal Psychology, 93,* 31-40.

Eisdorfer, C., Cohen, D., & Veith, R. (1980). *The psychopathology of aging.* Kalamazoo, MI: Upjohn Pharmaceuticals.

Eisdorfer, C., & Friedel, R. O. (1977). Psychotherapeutic drugs in aging. In M. Jarrick (Ed.), *Psychopharmacology in the practice of medicine.* New York: Appleton-Century-Crofts.

Ellis, A. (1970). *The essence of rational psychotherapy: A comprehensive approach to treatment.* New York: Institute for Rational Living.

Ellis, A., & Harper, R. A. (1961). *A guide to rational living.* Englewood Cliffs, NJ: Prentice-Hall.

Ford, J. M., & Pfefferbaum, A. (1980). The utility of brain potentials in determining age-related changes in central nervous system and cognitive functioning. In L. W. Poon (Ed.), *Aging in the 1980's: Psychological Issues* (pp. 115-124). Washington, DC: American Psychological Association.

Frost, N. R., & Clayton, P. J. (1977). Bereavement and psychiatric hospitalization. *Archives of General Psychiatry, 34,* 1172-1175.

Gallagher, D., & Thompson, L. W. (1981). *Depression in the elderly: A behavioral treatment manual.* Los Angeles: USC Press.

Garfield, S. L. (1978). Research on client variables in psychotherapy. In S. L. Garfield & A. E. Bergin (Eds.), *Handbook of psychotherapy and behavior change* (2d ed.) (pp. 191-232). New York: John Wiley and Sons.

Glick, D., Weiss, R. S., & Parkes, C. M. (1974). *The first year of bereavement.* New York: John Wiley and Sons.

Goldfarb, A. I. (1971). Group therapy with the old and aged. In H. I. Kaplan & B. J. Sadock (Eds.), *Comprehensive group psychotherapy* (pp. 623-642). Baltimore: Williams & Wilkins.

Greenblatt, M. (1978). The grieving spouse. *American Journal of Psychiatry, 135,* 43-47.

Hicks, R., Funkenstein, H. H., Dysken, M. W., & Davis, J. M. (1980). Geriatric psychopharmacology. In J. E. Birren & R. B. Sloane (Eds.), *Handbook of mental health and aging* (pp. 745-774). Englewood Cliffs, NJ: Prentice-Hall.

Jacobs, S., & Ostfeld, A. (1977). An epidemiological review of the mortality of bereavement. *Psychosomatic Medicine, 39,* 344-357.

Karacan, I., Salis, P. J., & Williams, R. L. (1978). The role of the sleep laboratory in diagnosis and treatment of impotence. In R. L. Williams & I. Karacan (Eds.), *Sleep disorders: Diagnosis and treatment* (pp. 353-382). New York: John Wiley and Sons.

Kaszniak, A. W., & Allender, J. (1985). Psychological assessment of depression in older adults. In G. M. Chaisson-Stewart (Ed.), *Depression in the elderly: An interdisciplinary approach* (pp. 107-160). New York: John Wiley and Sons.

Kaszniak, A. W., Sadeh, M., & Stern, L. Z. (1985). Differentiating depression from organic brain syndromes in older age. In G. M. Chaisson-Stewart (Ed.), *Depression in the elderly: An interdisciplinary approach* (pp. 161-192). New York: John Wiley and Sons.

Kraus, M. J., & Lilienfeld, S. (1959). Some epidemiological aspects of high mortality rate in the young widowed group. *Journal of Chronic Disease, 10,* 207-217.

Kuiper, N. A., Olinger, L. J., & MacDonald, N. R. (1983). Depressive schemata and the processing of personal and social information. In L. B. Alloy (Ed.), *Cognitive processes in depression.* New York: Guilford Press.

Lambert, M. J., & DeJulio, S. S. (1978, March). *The relative importance of client, therapist, and technique variables as predictors of psychotherapy outcome: The place of therapist "nonspecific" factors.* Paper presented at the annual meeting of the Division of Psychotherapy, American Psychological Association, Scottsdale, AZ.

Lazarus, R. S. (1984). On the primacy of affect. *American Psychologist, 39,* 124-129.

Lewis, J. M., & Johansen, K. H. (1982). Resistances to psychotherapy with the elderly. *American Journal of Psychotherapy, 36,* 497-504.

Lieberman, M. A., Yalom, I. D., & Miles, M. B. (1973). *Encounter groups: First facts.* New York: Basic Books.

Linsk, N., Howe, M. W., & Pinkston, E. M. (1975). Behavioral group work in a home for the aged. *Social Work, 20,* 454-463.

Lopez, M. A. (1980). Social skills training with institutionalized elderly: Effects of pre-counseling, structuring and overlearning on skill acquisition and transfer. *Journal of Counseling Psychology, 27,* 286-293.

Luborsky, L., Singer, B., & Luborsky, L. (1975). Comparative studies of psychotherapies: Is it true that "everyone has won and all must have prizes"? *Archives of General Psychiatry, 32,* 995-1008.

Maddison, D. (1968). The relevance of conjugal bereavement for preventive psychiatry. *British Journal of Medical Psychology, 41,* 223-233.

Marris, P. (1974). *Loss and change.* New York: Pantheon Books.

Mayerson, N. H. (1984). Preparing clients for group therapy: A critical review and theoretical formulation. *Clinical Psychology Review, 4,* 191-213.

Mayeux, R. (1982). Depression and dementia in Parkinson's disease. In C. D. Marsden & S. Fahn (Eds.), *Movement disorders* (pp. 75-95). London: Butterworth.

Meichenbaum, D. (1977). *Cognitive-behavior modification: An integrated approach.* New York: Plenum.

O'Neil, P. M., & Calhoun, K. S. (1975). Sensory deficits and behavioral deterioration in senescence. *Journal of Abnormal Psychology, 84,* 579.

Orchik, D. J. (1981). Peripheral auditory problems and the aging process. In D. S. Beasley & G. A. Davis (Eds.), *Aging: Communication processes and disorders* (pp. 243-255). New York: Grune and Stratton.

Parkes, C. M. (1964). The effects of bereavement on physical and mental health: A study of the case records of widows. *British Medical Journal, 2,* 274-279.

Parkes, C. M. (1972). *Bereavement: Studies of grief in adult life.* New York: International Universities Press.

Parloff, M. B., Waskow, I. E., & Wolfe, B. E. (1978). Research on therapist variables in relation to process and outcome. In S. L. Garfield & A. E. Bergin (Eds.), *Handbook of psychotherapy and behavior change* (2d ed.) (pp. 233-282). New York: John Wiley and Sons.

Paykel, E. S., Flenninger, R., & Watson, J. P. (1982). Psychiatric side effects of antihypertensive drugs other than reserpine. *Journal of Clinical Psychopharmacology, 2,* 14-39.

Pollock, G. H. (1977). The mourning process and creative organizational change. *Journal of the Psychoanalytic Association, 25,* 3-34.

Price, L. J., Fein, G., & Feinberg, I. (1980). Neuropsychological assessment of cognitive function in the elderly. In L. W. Poon (Ed.), *Aging in the 1980's: Psychological issues* (pp. 78-85). Washington, DC: American Psychological Association.

Rees, D. W., & Lutkins, S. G. (1967). Mortality of bereavement. *British Medical Journal, 4,* 13-16.

Romaniuk, M., McAuley, W. J., & Arling, G. (1983). An examination of the prevalence of mental disorders among the elderly in the community. *Journal of Abnormal Psychology, 92,* 458-467.

Rush, A. J., Beck, A. T., Kovacs, M., & Hollon, S. (1977). Comparative efficacy of cognitive therapy and pharmacotherapy in the treatment of depressed outpatients. *Cognitive Therapy and Research, 1,* 17-37.

Rush, A. J., Beck, A. T., Kovacs, M., Weissenburger, J., & Hollon, S. D. (1982). Comparison of the effects of cognitive therapy and pharmacotherapy on hopelessness and self-concept. *American Journal of Psychiatry, 139,* 862-866.

Sank, L. I., & Shaffer, C. S. (1984). *A therapist's manual for cognitive behavior therapy.* New York: Plenum Press.

Shapiro, D. A., & Shapiro, D. (1982). Meta-analysis of comparative therapy outcome studies: A replication and refinement. *Psychological Bulletin, 92,* 581-604.

Silverman, J. S., Silverman, J. A., & Eardley, D. A. (1984). Do maladaptive attitudes cause depression? *Archives of General Psychiatry, 41,* 28-32.

Simons, A. D., Garfield, S. L., & Murphy, G. E. (1984). The process of change in cognitive therapy and pharmacotherapy for depression. *Archives of General Psychiatry, 41,* 45-51.

Smith, M. L., Glass, G. V., & Miller, T. I. (1980). *The benefits of psychotherapy.* Baltimore: Johns Hopkins University Press.

Steinbrueck, S. M., Maxwell, S. E., & Howard, G. S. (1983). A meta-analysis of psychotherapy and drug therapy in the treatment of unipolar depression with adults. *Journal of Consulting and Clinical Psychology, 51,* 856-863.

Stenback, A. (1980). Depression and suicidal behavior in old age. In J. E. Birren & R. B. Sloan (Eds.), *Handbook of mental health and aging* (pp. 616-652). Englewood Cliffs, NJ: Prentice-Hall.

Taulbee, L. R. (1978). Reality orientation: A therapeutic group activity for elderly persons. In I. M. Burnside (Ed.), *Working with the elderly: Group processes and techniques* (pp. 206-218). North Scituate, MA: Duxbury.

Terry, R., & Katzman, R. (1983). Senile dementia of the Alzheimer's type: Defining a disease. In R. Katzman & R. Terry (Eds.), *The neurology of aging* (pp. 51-84). Philadelphia: F. A. Davis.

Tomlinson, B. E. (1982). Plagues, tangles and Alzheimer's disease. *Psychological Medicine, 12,* 449.

Troll, L. E., & Nowak, C. (1976). "How old are you?"—The question of age bias in the counseling of adults. *Counseling Psychologist, 6,* 41-44.

Vachon, M. L. S. (1976). Grief and bereavement following the death of a spouse. *Canadian Psychiatric Association Journal, 21,* 35-44.

Webb, W. B. (1982). Sleep in older persons: Sleep structures of 50- to 60-year-old men and women. *Journal of Gerontology, 37,* 581-586.

Weiner, M. B., & Weinstock, C. S. (1979-80). Group processes of community elderly as measured by tape recordings, group tempo, and group evaluation. *International Journal of Aging and Human Development, 10,* 177-185.

Whitlock, F. A. (1982). *Symptomatic affective disorders*. Sydney, Australia: Academic Press.

Yost, E. B., Allender, J. A., Beutler, L. E., & Chaisson-Stewart, G. M. (1983). Developments in the treatment of depression among the elderly. *Arizona Medicine, 15*, 402–407.

Yost, E. B., & Corbishley, M. A. (1985). Group therapy. In G. M. Chaisson-Stewart (Ed.), *Depression in the elderly: An interdisciplinary approach* (pp. 288–315). New York: John Wiley and Sons.

Young, M., Benjamin, B., & Wallis, C. (1963). The mortality of widowers. *Lancet, 2*, 254–256.

Zajonc, R. B. (1984). On the primacy of affect. *American Psychologist, 39*, 117–123.

Author Index

140 Author Index

Hicks, R., 4
Hollon, S. D., 6, 7, 40
Howard, G. S., 7
Howe, M. W., 26

Jacobs, S., 2
Johansen, K. H., 4
Johnson, C., 19

Karacan, I., 3, 37
Kaszniak, A. W., 1, 36, 37, 38
Katzman, R., 3
Kovacs, M., 7, 40
Kramer, N., 14
Kraus, M. J., 2
Kuiper, N. A., 7

Lambert, M. J., 54
Lawson, I., 4
Lazarus, R. S., 7
Lewis, J. M., 4
Lieberman, M. A., 46, 120, 121
Lilienfeld, S., 2
Linsk, N., 26
Lipman, R. S., 10
Lopez, M. A., 19
Luborsky, L., 7
Lutkins, S. G., 2

MacDonald, N. R., 7
Maddison, D., 3
Marris, P., 3
Maurice, W. L., 3
Maxwell, S. E., 7
Mayerson, N. H., 41, 42, 53
Mayeux, R., 3
McCauley, W. J., 1
Meichenbaum, D., 9
Miles, M. B., 46, 120, 121
Miller, T. I., 6
Murphy, G. E., 7

Nowak, C., 4

Olinger, L. J., 7
O'Neil, P. M., 3

Orchik, D. J., 3
Ostfeld, A., 2

Parkes, C. M., 2, 3
Parloff, M. B., 41, 54
Paykel, E. S., 40
Pfefferbaum, A., 18
Pinkston, E. M., 26
Pollock, G. H., 2
Poon, L. W., 18
Price, L. J., 18

Raskind, M. A., 4
Rees, D. W., 2
Romaniuk, M., 1
Roth, D., 10
Rush, A. J., 7, 9, 11, 23, 34, 40

Sadeh, M., 3, 36, 37, 38
Salis, P. J., 3, 37
Sank, L. I., 10, 23
Shaffer, C. S., 10, 23
Shapiro, D., 6, 7
Shapiro, D. A., 6, 7
Shaw, B. F., 9, 11, 23, 34
Silverman, J. A., 7
Silverman, J. S., 7
Simons, A. D., 7
Singer, B., 7
Smith, M. L., 6
Steinbrueck, S. M., 7
Stenback, A., 37
Stern, L. Z., 3, 36, 37, 38

Taulbee, L. R., 15
Terry, R., 3
Thompson, L. W., 10
Tomlinson, B. E., 3
Troll, L. E., 4

Vachon, M. L. S., 3
Veith, R. C., 1, 2, 4
Verwoerdt, A., 2

Wallis, C., 2
Waskow, I. E., 54

Subject Index

About the Authors

Elizabeth B. Yost is Associate Professor, Department of Psychology, University of Arizona, and Research Associate, Department of Psychiatry, University of Arizona, College of Medicine. She received her Ph.D. in Counseling Psychology from the University of Oregon and worked at the Pennsylvania State University before moving to Arizona. She is coauthor of *Effective Personal and Career Decision Making*, of a chapter on group therapy in C. M. Chaisson-Stewart's *Depression in the Elderly: Concepts, Diagnosis and Intervention*, and of a book on career counseling to be published by Jossey-Bass.

Larry E. Beutler is Professor of Psychiatry and Psychology at the University of Arizona, College of Medicine. He received a Ph.D. from the University of Nebraska-Lincoln, is a diplomate of the American Board of Professional Psychology, Associate Editor of the *Journal of Consulting and Clinical Psychology*, and President-Elect of the Society for Psychotherapy Research. He is author of *Eclectic Psychotherapy: A Systematic Approach* and coeditor of *Special Problems in Child and Adolescent Behavior*.

M. Anne Corbishley is a doctoral candidate in Counseling and Guidance at the University of Arizona. She received her undergraduate degree from Oxford University, England, and her M.Ed. from the University of Arizona. She is coauthor of a chapter on group therapy in C. M. Chaisson-Stewart's *Depression in the Elderly: Concepts, Diagnosis and Intervention* and of a book on career counseling to be published by Jossey-Bass.Her dissertation research concerns sleep EEG variables as markers for depression in older adults.

James R. Allender is Assistant Clinical Professor at the University of Arizona, College of Medicine. He obtained his Ph.D. from the University of New Mexico in 1984. In addition to his work with depressed older adults, he has been involved in research and clinical work with patients with primary degenerative dementia, patients undergoing heart transplantation, and patients with eating disorders.

Psychology Practitioner Guidebooks

Editors
Arnold P. Goldstein, Syracuse University
Leonard Krasner, SUNY at Stony Brook
Sol L. Garfield, Washington University